EVALUATING
BEER

EVALUATING
BEER

EDITED BY

BREWERS PUBLICATIONS

 Brewers Publications, Boulder, Colorado USA

Evaluating Beer
Edited by Brewers Publications
Copyright ©1993 Association of Brewers Inc.

ISBN 0-937381-37-3

Published by Brewers Publications
a division of the Association of Brewers Inc.
PO Box 1679, Boulder, Colorado 80306-1679 USA
Tel. (303) 447-0816, FAX (303) 447-2825

Direct all inquiries/orders to the above address

Art direction and cover illustration by Vicki Hopewell.

TABLE OF CONTENTS

INTRODUCTION

J ust what is it that drew you to that unmistakable and uncompromising taste of fresh beer? Was it when your neighbor opened the door to a new world of unique taste through a homebrew? A sip of some beer you can't even remember the name of at that brewpub you stumbled on while vacationing last year? A plan to stretch the limits of what you used to call "good beer"?

Whatever the reasons, you know what you like and now you're hooked on making your beer even better or on learning how to *truly* judge the taste of the beer in front of you. Thanks to our industry-leading authors, you no longer have to think you need to be a brewing scientist to learn what you need to know — you're going to find answers to all your questions in this one reference book. This comprehensive collection meets the needs of beer enthusiasts, homebrewers, and professional brewers alike.

You may already know that sensory evaluation, which includes flavor profiling and off-flavor detection, focuses on the effect of variables on a beer. And maybe you have no question that your senses are the primary tools for evaluating beer. But do

Elizabeth Gold
Director,
Brewers Publications

you understand how to use the internationally recognized Beer Flavor Wheel or how to measure beer color? Are you able to use the American

Homebrewers Association beer competition score sheet to your advantage? Ever wonder how the Beer Judge Certification Program trains people to judge beer or how a beer is judged by the professionals?

Included in this book is a beer flavor terminology chart — one of the most complete flavor descriptor charts available. Without a doubt, it will enhance your understanding of the finite flavors possible in beer. You'll also learn what skews sensory perceptions as well as the history and chemical composition of beer flavor. Variables that effect beer flavor, including the influence of temperature, light, and ingredients, are thoroughly covered from different perspectives. You'll discover the factors of flavor tasting — evaluation, consistency, and isolating and correcting defects.

As you read these chapters, it will become clear to you that evaluation goes beyond simply asking if the beer in front of you is good or bad — it's learning how to determine which components of that beer make it different from others.

And that's only the beginning.

It's been an enlightening pleasure preparing this collection. Thanks to our authors and editors, David Logan and Dena Nishek, for their parts in bringing this book to you. I hope your next beer tastes better than your last, and after reading this book, you'll *certainly* know why it does or doesn't.

All the best,
Elizabeth Gold
Director, Brewers Publications

EVALUATING BEER

CHARLIE PAPAZIAN

I t's my beer, my taste, my opinion. So what do I care what anyone else thinks about my beer? I like it, it sells, and that's all that matters. What more do I need to know about my beer's taste and aroma?

If your thoughts run in this mode, you're about 15 years behind the times. Today, the way we evaluate beer has changed. Never before have so many brewers been so keenly interested in the characteristics of different beer styles and the flavor nuances of their own brews. Hundreds of beer styles are now being brewed. A new breed of educated consumer is tasting and evaluating beer with enthusiasm. Microbrewed and pubbrewed beers are in the eye of the public and professional evaluator alike giving them products to assess, compare, praise or scorn. But perhaps most important to the commerical brewer, beer evaluation gives information that can be used to maximize quality and minimize problems.

As well, homebrewers are a unique group of beer enthusiasts. Never before has there been such a large group of brewers having an interest in the characteristics of different beer styles and the flavor nuances of their own brews. Hundreds of beer styles are now being brewed. One brewer is more than likely to have a stock of homebrewed pale ale, stout, fruit beer, bock, steam and Munich Helles all at the same time. With a desire to learn and improve their own brews and those of others, homebrewers are learning to taste and evaluate beer with enthusiasm. Homebrewed beer has become the apple of the public's eye.

It has been a very long time since North America has seen such a variety of beer brewed with so many different philosophies and variations in brewing ingredients, processes, equipment systems and handling. Concomitant all of these variations there exists a wide variety of beer tastes, aromas, mouthfeels, sounds, visual qualities and overall impressions we believe are unique. Actually, these sensations are nothing new. They've all been experienced before. The difference today is that the scope of our knowledge lends itself to evaluating beers with a wide-angle lens, rather than with the narrow field of telephoto lens. In other words, today, with so many beer styles, we're taking a more informed approach to defining beer style characteristics and quality control.

Beer evaluation is a learned skill, which I will discuss later, but first let's consider the reasons why brewers need to know how to evaluate beer.

1. *To control quality and consistency.* For example, every large brewery in North America has a regular program of evaluating its beer for the sole purpose of ascertaining that its quality is consistent from batch to batch. The breweries are not necessarily trying to detect unusual flavors in order to identify their origins. Instead, beer evaluators are specially trained to evaluate usually just one style of beer — the brewery's own brand.

2. *To be able to describe a given beer.* How does your beer taste? "This beer tastes good (or bad)." "It's a party beer." "It's less filling." "The one beer to have when you want more than one." These

generic descriptions just don't cut it any more if you want to identify for yourself or communicate your beer's character to other beer enthusiasts.

And also, because of the proliferation of beer styles being brewed in North America, a language has developed over the last decade that effectively communicates the characteristics of beer. If you can evaluate your beer's strong or weak points and describe them accurately, you may be able to improve the character of your beer in a way that results in exactly what you want.

3. *To score and/or judge in a competition*. Beer competitions are becoming more and more popular. Hundreds of beer enthusiasts and brewers are spending a great deal of time learning to evaluate beer and determine a winner in a contest. Whether or not you agree with the principle of competition is irrelevant. It *is* being done. And the people who are evaluating beers for this purpose are getting better at it. This is a specialized perspective on the art and science of evaluation and one that has taken the direction of blending objectivity with subjectivity. The evaluators or judges use scientific and technical terms in objectively assessing beer qualities and assessing them for drinkability and appropriateness to a style.

4. *To define styles*. For every beer you brew, there is born a style. The skill of the brewer, combined with the tools at his or her disposal, make for the individuality of any glass of beer. So why do definitions of "styles" emerge when we take pride in our own uniqueness? One reason is so we can communicate in a descriptive word or two the general character of our beers. So we can help develop traditions, enthusiasm and reasons to argue about better or worse, too malty or bitter. We define styles to create identification.

5. *To develop terms and definitions as tools to describe styles of beer.* In order to use these tools, we must learn how to evaluate beer in a specific way for a specific reason. Evaluating a beer's character for appropriateness of style is a specialized skill and one that requires patience, time and appreciation for all kinds of beer. An educated and properly trained evaluator may evaluate a given beer in any style, whether the taste is preferred personally or not.

6. *To detect problems and improve your own or someone else's beer.* This is perhaps the most challenging of all reasons to evaluate beer. Not only does the evaluator need to identify any one of hundreds of characters, but he or she also needs to identify the source of the character. If you are able to evaluate a beer's flavor, aroma, appearance, mouthfeel and after-taste — and then identify the source of these characters, you can control, adjust and improve the quality of your brew.

SIX SENSES FOR EVALUATION

Sophisticated equipment can be used to measure your beer to no end, right down to the last little molecule, the kinds and amounts of constituents that could be in your beer. Technological evaluation may augment but never replace the objective and subjective findings of a trained evaluator.

The human senses of taste, smell, sight, hearing and touch can be trained as very effective tools to evaluate beer. But it takes patience, development of confidence, time, and above all, humility. It takes practice. I know. I have watched hundreds of beer enthusiasts and brewers improve their evaluation skills over the years, to such a degree that they enjoy beer more and brew better beer.

Sight. You can tell a lot about a beer by just looking at it while it's in the bottle or glass.

Excessive head space in the the bottle is an indication that air content may be high. This tells you what oxidized flavor and aroma characters may follow. A surface deposit ringing the inside of the bottle's neck is a clear indication of bacterial or wild yeast contamination. In this case, sourness and excessive acidity may result. Gushing (another visual experience) also may be the result of bacterial or wild yeast contamination.

Sediment in a filtered beer may indicate an old, stale beer. Watch out for gushing. Sediment also may indicate precipitation of oxalates, a result of the brewing water lacking appropriate brewing salts — a sure cause of gushing. Hazy beer can be the result of bacterial or yeast infection. Chill haze, a precipitate of a tannin-protein compound, doesn't affect the flavor, but it can be remedied when identified.

When poured into a brandy snifter, high-alcohol beers such as doppelbocks and barley wines verify their strength by showing their "legs" on the sides of the glass. "Legs" refer to a coating of liquid that concentrates into streams as it runs down the side of a glass.

The complete lack of foam stability in a glass of a newly-poured beer (assuming the glass is beer-clean) may be an indication that the beer is stale, old, and oxidized.

Hearing. It takes a lot of attention, but for an experienced evaluator, that sound upon opening — of gas escaping from a bottle — is music of specific tones for different volumes of carbon dioxide.

Smell. The most sensitive of our senses and the most telling is our sense of smell. Assessing a beer's aroma should be a quick experience. Our smell "detectors" quickly become anesthetized to whatever we are smelling. For example, you may walk into a room and smell the strong aroma of coffee perking. Five minutes later, the smell lingers just as strongly, but you don't notice it.

Our smell "detectors" reside in a side pocket of dead air along our nasal passage. In order to assess aromas, we must take air into this side pocket. The most effective way of doing this is to create a lot of turbulence in the nasal passage. Several short, strong sniffs or long, deep sniffs help get the aromatic molecules of vaporized beer smells into this pocket. Then our memory and current experience combine to identify what we smell.

Getting the aromas out of the beer doesn't happen so easily. It is best done with beers warmed to at least 45 to 50 degrees F (7 to 10 degrees C) so that volatiles and aromatic compounds will change form from liquid to gas. Swirl a half-full glass of beer to release the carbon dioxide bubbles into the air, carrying with them other aromatic gases.

Note that some constituents of beer flavor and aroma are so volatile that they virtually disappear from beer within a matter of a few minutes. This is the case with some sulfur-based compounds like DMS (a sweet-cornlike aroma), giving the beer an entirely different smell and taste after it has sat out for a time and disappeared.

Taste. The tongue is the main flavor assessor in the mouth. It is mapped out in four distinct areas. Bitter is experienced at the back of the tongue. Sweet at the front tip of the tongue, and salt and sour on the sides of the tongue. It is interesting to note that 15 to 20 percent of Americans confuse sour with bitter and vice versa. Clarify this for yourself by noting where on the tongue you are experiencing the taste sensation.

"Chew" the beer when evaluating. Because different areas of the tongue experience various flavors, you must coat all of your tongue and mouth with the beer and then swallow. Beer evaluators — don't spit it out! It is important to assess the experience of swallowing beer for its aftertaste and so that all parts of the mouth are exposed. There are flavor receptors on the sides, back and roof of the mouth independent of the tongue.

Touch and Feel. Your mouth most importantly senses the texture of the beer. Often called body, the texture of beer can be full-bodied or light-bodied as extremes. Astringency (also related to huskiness and graininess) can also be assessed by mouthfeel. It is not a flavor, but rather a dry, puckery feeling, exactly like chewing on the skin of a grape. This astringent sensation most often comes from tannins excessively extracted from grains as a result of oversparging, sparging with overheated water or having a high pH. Sometimes astringency can be the result of milling your grains too finely.

Other sensations that can be felt are oily, cooling — as in menthollike, burning and temperature.

Pleasure. This is our sixth sense. This is the close-your-eyes drinkability, the overall impression, the memorableness of the beer. No evaluation is complete without this final assessment. Is the beer pleasurable? Would you want another? This is the assessment and the evaluation that turned you into a brewer or beer enthusiast, isn't it?

Our senses, like a $100,000 machine plugged into the electric socket, are sensitive to power surges, brown-outs and other ups and downs that influence the show. Our own genetic makeup can affect our ability to detect or not detect certain chemical compounds' aromas and flavors. Also, our health is a very significant factor. Two to three days before we show the first outward symptoms of a cold or flu, our taste buds may go completely haywire. Taste panels that make million-dollar decisions consider this and do not rely on just one taster but on several in order to account for temporary inaccuracies of perception.

Finally, the environment in which we assess should be comforting and not distracting. Smoke, loud music and unusual lighting should be avoided.

SOME FACTORS INFLUENCING THE CHARACTER OF BEER

Here is a thumbnail sketch of some of the more common factors influencing the character of beer.

INGREDIENTS

Malt — contributes color, mouthfeel, sweetness, level of astringency, and alcohol strength.

Hops — contributes bitterness level, flavor, aroma, sometimes can contribute to a metallic character, can be citrusy or floral in aroma.

Yeast — strains and environment can affect diacetyl (buttery-butterscotch) levels; hydrogen sulfide (rotten egg smell) particularly in bottle-conditioned beer; phenolic character including clove; plasticlike aroma and flavor; fruitiness and esters.

Water — chlorination can result in harsh chlorophenolic (plasticlike) aroma and flavor. Saltiness can be caused by the excess of certain mineral salts. High pH can result in harsh bitterness from unwanted extraction from grain and/or hops.

PROCESS

Milling — grain too finely crushed can result in husky-grainy and/or astringent character.

Mashing — temperature can affect level of sweetness, alcohol, body or mouthfeel, astringency.

Temperature — during fermentation it can affect level of estery-fruitiness; slow chilling of wort can increase DMS (sweet-cornlike character) levels.

Lautering — temperature of sparge water can affect level of tannins and subsequent phenols detected in finished beer.

Boiling — short boiling times or non-vigorous boils can result in high DMS levels; vigorous boiling precipitates proteins out of solution. Also extracts hop flavors.

Fermentation — at high temperatures can cause fusel alcohols and/or solventlike characters; cooling regime can elevate or decrease diacetyl levels in finished beer.

EQUIPMENT

Sanitation — Lack of sanitation can result in bacterial or wild yeast contamination causing unusual effects on flavor, aroma, appearance, texture; residues of sanitizer can contribute to medicinal-phenolic character.

Design — Equipment design, from kettles, fermenters and plumbing, can grossly affect boiling regime, fermentation cycles, cleanability; the same combination of ingredients can be affected by different configurations and sizes of equipment.

Scaling batch size up or down in brew size can have significant and unforeseen effects on character of beer.

HANDLING

Temperature — warm temperature grossly affects the freshness of beer; warm temperatures speed up the oxidation process.

Oxygen — destroys the flavor of finished beer. Oxygen combines with beer compounds and alcohol to produce negative flavors and aromas described as winy, stale, sherrylike, papery, wet cardboard, rotten vegetables, or rotten pineapple.

Light — ultraviolet wavelengths of light photochemically react with hop compounds to produce a lightstruck skunky character. Green or clear glass bottles offer no protection.

Agitation — rough handling enhances the oxidation process.

DESCRIPTOR DEFINITIONS FOR SCORING USED BY THE AMERICAN HOMEBREWERS ASSOCIATION

Acetaldehyde: Green applelike aroma, byproduct of fermentation.

Alcoholic: The general effect of ethanol and higher alcohols. Tastes warming.

Astringent: Drying, puckering (like chewing on a grape skin); feeling often associated with sourness. Tannin. Most often derived from boiling of grains, long mashes, oversparging or sparging with hot water.

Bitter: Basic taste associated with hops; Braunhefe or malt husks. Sensation experienced on back of tongue.

Chill Haze: Haze caused by precipitation of protein-tannin compound at cold temperatures. Does not affect flavor. Reduction of proteins or tannins in brewing or fermenting will reduce haze.

Chlorophenolic: Caused by chemical combination of chlorine and organics. Detectable in parts per billion. Aroma is unique but similar to plasticlike phenolic. Avoid using chlorinated water.

Clean: Lacking off-flavors.

Cooked Vegetable/ Cabbagelike: Aroma and flavor often due to long lag times and wort spoilage bacteria that later are killed by alcohol produced in fermentation.

Diacetyl-Buttery: Described as buttery, butterscotch.

DMS (dimethyl sulfide): A sweet-cornlike aroma/flavor. Can be attributed to malt, short or non-vigorous boiling of wort, slow wort chilling or in extreme cases bacterial infection.

Fruity-Estery: Similar to banana, raspberry, pear, apple or strawberry flavor; may include other fruity-estery flavors. Often accentuated with higher temperature fermentations and certain yeast strains.

Grainy: Raw grain flavor. Cereallike. Some amounts are appropriate in some beer styles.

Hoppy: Characteristic odor of the essential oil of hops. Does not include hop bitterness.

Husky: see Astringent.

Lightstruck: Having the characteristic smell of a skunk, caused by exposure to light. Some hops can have a very similar character.

Metallic: Caused by exposure to metal. Also described as tinny, coins, bloodlike. Check your brewpot and caps.

Oxidized-Stale: Develops in the presence of oxygen as beer ages or is exposed to high temperatures; wet cardboard, papery, rotten vegetable or pineapple, winy, sherry, uric acid. Often coupled with an increase in sour, harsh or bitter. The more aeration in bottling, filtering and transferring, or air in headspace, the more quickly a beer oxidizes. Warm temperatures dramatically accelerate oxidation.

Phenolic: Can be any one or a combination of a medicinal, plastic, electrical fire, Listerinelike, Band-Aidlike, smoky, clovelike aroma or flavor. Most often caused by wild strains of yeast or bacteria. Can be extracted from grains (see Astringent). Sanitizing residues left in equipment can contribute.

Solventlike: Flavor and aromatic character of certain alcohols, often caused by high fermentation temperatures. Like acetone, lacquer thinner.

Sour-Acidic: Pungent aroma, sharpness of taste. Basic taste like vinegar or lemon; tart. Typically associated with lactic or acetic acid. Can be the result of bacterial infection through contamination or the use of citric acid. Sensation experienced on sides of tongue.

Salty: Flavor associated with table salt. Sensation experienced on sides of tongue. Can be caused from presence of too much sodium chloride, calcium chloride or magnesium sulfate (Epsom salts); brewing salts.

Sweet: Basic taste associated with sugar. Sensation experienced on front tip of tongue.

Sulfurlike (H_2S; **hydrogen sulfide**): Rotten eggs, burning matches, flatulence. A byproduct with certain strains of yeast. Fermentation temperature can be a factor of intensity. Diminishes with age. Most evident with bottle-conditioned beer.

Yeasty: Yeastlike flavor. Often due to strains of yeast in suspension or beer sitting on sediment too long.

BEER AROMA RECOGNITION GUIDELINES – Substances That Can Be Added to Beer for Training Purposes

Mielgaard Ref.#	General Descriptor	Technical Descriptor	Substance Used for Recognition Training	Amt. to Use in 12 oz. Beer	Amt. to Use in One Quart Beer
0110	Alcoholic	Alcohol	Ethanol	15 ml	40 ml
0111	Clove	Spicy	Eugenol / Allspice	40 mg / 2 g	106 mg / 5 g
0112	Winy	Fusely, Vinous	Gallo Chablis	3 fl. oz.	8 fl. oz.
0123	Solventlike	Acetone	Lacquer Thinner	0.02 ml	0.05 ml
0133	Estery, Fruity, Solvent	Ethyl Acetate	Ethyl Acetate	0.007 ml or 7 mg	0.019 ml or 7 mg
0150	Green Apples	Acetaldehyde	Acetaldehyde	0.002 ml or 2 mg	0.005 ml or 5 mg
0220	Sherry	Sherry	Sherry	2.5 fl. oz.	6.5 fl. oz.
0224	Almond, Nutty	Nutty	Benzaldehyde / Almond Extract	0.002 ml or 2 mg / 4 drops	0.005 ml or 5 mg / 11 drops
0503	Medicinal, Bandaidlike, Plasticlike	Phenolic	Phenol	0.003 ml or 3 mg	0.01 ml or 10 mg
0620	Butter, Butterscotch	Diacetyl	Diacetyl / Butter-flavor Extract	0.0001 ml or 0.1 mg / 4 drops	0.00027 ml or 0.27 mg / 11 drops
0710	Sulfury	Sulfitic, Sulfur dioxide	Sodium or Potassium Metabisulfite	2 mg	5 mg
0721	Skunky, Lightstruck	Skunky	Beer exposed to light		
0732	Sweet Corn, Cabbage	Dimethylsulfide/DMS	Dimethylsulfide/DMS	0.00003 ml or 30 mg	0.0001 ml or 100 mg
0800	Stale, Cardboard	Stale, Oxidation	Heat sample for one week at 90-100°F		
0910	Sour/Vinegar	Acetic (acid)	White Vinegar	30 ml	100 ml
0920	Sour/Lactic	Lactic (acid)	Lactic Acid	0.4 ml	1.1 ml

Substances are to be used for aroma recognition only. Do not drink doctored beer samples, some are poisonous. Developed by Greg Noonan, Vermont Pub and Brewery of Burlington, and Charlie Papazian, Association of Brewers. (Much of this data is from Dr. Morten Meilgaard's work.)

THE FLAVOR OF BEER

MORTEN C. MEILGAARD, D.SC., F.I. BREW.

The past 50 years have seen an enormous growth in our knowledge about flavor and in flavor research. One could argue, borrowing a term from atomic physics, that we have reached a point of having acquired a critical mass of accurate scientific information about the flavor elements of beer. It is time to stand back and see what we have. What I propose to do is take the flavor apart, split it into its elements, then try to define the individual elements one by one. Then I'll review which are the desirable and some interesting not-so-desirable elements; I won't spend much time on the beer faults except for oxidation flavor. Next, I propose to put the flavor together again. I'll try to show how the world's great beers are put together, the roles played by tradition, invention, and necessity. Finally I'll try to define which are the factors that are shaping the newer types, the low-calorie, dry, non-alcohol, and today's designer beers.

RESEARCH PLAN TO DISCOVER THE FLAVOR ELEMENTS OF BEER

At the time this study was begun, it had become clear that to make any headway with problems in flavor research, one must attack them from two sides, that of the taster, and the chemist. The chemists' approach had already produced lists of hundreds of volatile and nonvolatile compounds present in beer, but little was known about the flavor type and the relative flavor strength of each, and there were no standard taste testing methods for describing flavor type. The first research plan therefore had to use the method of the taster, Table 1.

Research Plan 1 was drawn up in collaboration between the MBAA, the EBC and the ASBC and it led to interesting and fruitful studies in which more than 100 members of the three organizations participated (see later). In parallel, Plan 2 was drawn up for the method of the chemist. The ASBC and the EBC sponsored the work of purifying and determining thresholds for some forty compounds that were candidates for use as refer-

TABLE 1. Plan of the Investigation

Research Plan 1: Method of the Taster	Research Plan 2: Method of the Chemist	Research Plan 3: Combined Approach
1. Develop a terminology system which has a name for each of the individually recognizable flavor notes in beer.	1. Make a running inventory of compounds discovered in beer (more than 900 to date, not counting isomers).	1. Discover how the flavor intensity of added substances varies with the concentration added.
2. Develop a system of reference substances for these flavor notes, with methods of purification and directions of use for each.	2. Determine the concentration of each in various types of beer.	2. By adding mixtures of compounds, discover the rules of flavor interaction in mixtures.
3. Develop methods of analytical taste testing, in particular: • threshold tests; • descriptive tests; • scaling methods for flavor intensity.	3. Determine or estimate a rough flavor threshold for each so as to discover those likely to be flavor active) perhaps 100, as it turned out).	3. Conduct descriptive testing and detailed chemical analysis of numerous beers.
	4. Obtain or synthesize those compounds likely to be flavor active.	4. Analyze the data by multivariate statistical procedures.
	5. Purify each to a state of sensory purity, then determine its threshold in a not-too-flavorful beer.	5. Develop hypotheses; test compounds having the expected type of flavor; confirm or reject the hypotheses.

ence substances for the terminology system. Approximately 180 additional compounds were studied in the author's laboratories at Cerveceria Cuauhtémoc and at the Stroh Brewery Company. Finally in Plan 3 the two approaches were combined. Results from these studies have been published and will only be repeated here to the extent they are needed in the discussion.

THE TASTER'S APPROACH: METHODS DEVELOPMENT, RESULTS

FLAVOR TERMINOLOGY

The international system of terminology has fourteen classes, forty-six first-tier terms and seventy-six second-tier terms. One could ask, does this mean that to a specialist, the flavor of beer consists of 122 separately definable elements? Perhaps not quite: on the one hand, one should bear in mind that a major part of the terms represent off-flavors that are rarely present and on the other hand, that there are weak areas where the system does not describe all the flavor notes, for example the area of stale flavors, and the mouthfeel sector. For the latter, Langstaff et al. have suggested several promising terms. Further, many of the desirable terms occur only in specialty beers such as Belgian Lambic or Bavarian Rauchbier. For practical purposes one could say that there are more than 100 separately identifiable flavor elements that a good taster should know; about forty of these are common and are present in most beers; the rest are either flavor faults or are characteristics of specialty beers.

ANALYTICAL TASTE TESTING

The expert analytical panel is the main tool for taking flavor apart. We use the panel members as measuring instruments. As such they are highly

variable and greatly exposed to bias. The sensitivity
to smells or tastes of even a trained panelist varies
plus or minus 30 to 40 percent or more from one
test to the next. Worse, "perception of the world is
not a passive process, but an active and selective
one. An observer records only those elements of a
complex process that he can readily see and associate as meaningful. The rest he eliminates even if
they are staring him in the face" (Gregson). As
O'Mahony et al. have pointed out, a critical stage is
that of concept formation. Take the colors as an
example: at an early age we each learn the same
concept of "redness"; we encounter many shades of
orange, red and brown and we learn which can be
called "red." However, in the case of smells and
tastes, learning is not systematic, and as a result,
different people have very different concepts. It follows that strong controls are needed if one is to
obtain reproducible verdicts. Table 2 shows some of
the traps which lurk below the surface to cause bias
in sensory verdicts. Each needs to be anticipated
and guarded against in the setup of the panel and
the tests. Above all, we need an intelligent and
experienced sensory analyst. One who can teach the
agreed flavor concepts and cause them to be identified and recorded whenever they are present.

CONSUMER TESTING

In consumer testing, all the same pitfalls exist,
plus many, many more, and the cost per test is 50
to 100 times higher. Some of the factors one needs
to critically define are listed in Table 3. For example, the purpose: is it a maintenance test, an optimization study or a new product development test?
If it is a product development test, is it an early
evaluation of a concept, a more advanced comparison of several prototypes, or a full-scale test of a

proposed new product? Table 3 is by no means exhaustive; good consumer testing requires a competent and seasoned organizer, otherwise results can be very misleading.

Assume for the sake of discussion that we want to find out which flavor elements "drive" preference. We then need to critically select the target consumer group, say legal age to thirty-four who made a purchase of a designer beer in the past two weeks. Is Central Location or Home Use the best? We need to critically define product presentation: for example, how do you avoid dirty glasses or warm beer in a home use test? Above all, one needs to use imagination when planning the setup and the questions. One may include items like image attributes, or an annoyance scale, or a purchase intent scale. Consumers use flavor terms in strange and nonreproducible ways, so flavor attributes can only be studied in roundabout ways, for example, by comparing with other products or by presenting examples. Multivariate analysis methods are needed, but they are tricky: test several on your data, then repeat and repeat until findings are secure.

THRESHOLD TESTING

Methods of defining and calculating sensory thresholds were recently reviewed by ASTM Task Group E18.04.25 and its conclusions were reported to the ASBC. The range of thresholds found for compounds added to beer is truly astounding: from 14,000 ppm for ethanol, to 0.07 ppt for tertiary amyl mercaptan, or 2×10^{12} or two trillion times. It follows (i) that high chemical purity, even 99.9999 percent, does not guarantee sensory purity, and (ii) that large numbers of compounds have thresholds well below the detection limit of most gas chromatographs, approximately 10 ppt. In

TABLE 2. Some Factors Which Cause Bias in Sensory Verdicts

A. PHYSIOLOGICAL FACTORS

Factor	Description	Examples
1. Adaptation	A decrease in or change in sensitivity to a given stimulus as a result of continued exposure to that stimulus or a similar one.	A subject, having tasted a set of bitter beers, is unable to properly score the bitterness in a less bitter sample.
2. Cross-Adaptation	Adaptation caused by previous exposure to a different substance.	Insensitivity to the sweetness of sugar caused by previous exposure to another sweetener.
3. Cross-Potentiation	Positive adaptation (or facilitation) caused by previous exposure to a substance of opposite flavor.	An observer having been exposed to a sweet solution perceives more bitterness in a subsequent bitter solution.
4. Enhancement	Effect of the presence of one substance increasing the perceived intensity of another presented simultaneously.	Amyl alcohols enhance the perceptions of the rose flavor of phenylethanol.
5. Synergy	Effect of the simultaneous presence of two or more substances increasing the perceived intensity of the mixture above the sum of the intensities of the components.	Although cases of apparent synergy are often reported, the author does not know of a really convincing example.
6. Suppression, Masking	Effect of the presence of one substance decreasing the perceived intensity of another presented simultaneously.	A high level of bitterness + hop aroma is said to mask oxidation flavor.

B. PSYCHOLOGICAL FACTORS

Factor	Description	Examples
1. Expectation Error	Information deliberately or inadvertently supplied with the sample may trigger preconceived ideas.	A panelist hearing that overaged product has been returned to the plant will tend to detect aged flavors in the day's test.
2. Error of Habituation	Tendency to repeat the same response when samples show low levels of variation.	Subjects who miss a developing trend in samples tasted for quality control.
3. Stimulus Error	Observer is influenced by irrelevant criteria suggesting difference, such as the style or color of the container.	Wines in screw-capped bottles tend to be rated lower than wines in corked bottles.
4. Logical Error	Observer modifies a verdict because two or more characteristics of the sample are associated in his mind.	A darker beer may be rated more flavorful. A darker mayonnaise may be rated more stale than it is.

5. Halo Effect	Observer, having formed a low (or high) overall opinion of a sample, gives low (high) ratings to many attributes, including some which do not deserve this.	A beer which receives a high overall rating also tends to be rated high on freshness and hop aroma, and low on oxidation flavor and astringency.
6. Order of Presentation Effects:		
Contrast Effect	A sample, preceded by another of contrasting character, may receive a more extreme rating than if it had been evaluated monadically.	February 40°F-weather in Minneapolis is a heat wave, in Miami it is a cold spell; a bland sample presented after a flavorful one may be rated blander than it would have if presented alone.
Group Effect	One sample presented together with a group of samples of contrasting character may be rated closer to the group than if it had been evaluated alone.	A bland sample in the midst of many flavorful ones may be rated more flavorful.
Error of Central Tendency	Samples presented near the center of a set tend to be preferred over those at the end.	The three mid samples in a set of five tend to be rated higher in hop aroma, lower in oxidation flavor.
Pattern Effect	Panelists are quick to detect any repeated pattern in the order or manner of presentation of samples.	If flavorful samples are often served late in the test, panelists will return higher ratings for the flavor intensity of samples presented late.
Time Error/ Positional bias	Subtle changes of attitude occur between the sample presented first and that presented last. The direction of these effect varies with circumstances.	In short tests the first sample is rated higher because of anticipation or thirst; in long tests (home placement) the last sample tends to be preferred.
7. Mutual Suggestion	The response is influenced by other panelists' reactions.	Panelists saying "eeech," scratching their heads or taking longer or shorter than usual.
8. Lack of Motivation	Panelist takes less care than usual, or less care than other panelists.	Less care taken to discern a subtle difference, or to search for a proper term, or to be consistent in assigning scores.
9. Capriciousness vs. Timidity	Panelist exaggerates use of extremes of scale vs. sticks to a narrow band in center of scale.	Caprecious panelists exert more than due influence on panel's results while more careful and painstaking panelists exert too little influence.

TABLE 3. Some Factors Which Need Consideration In Consumer Tests

A. PRODUCT MAINTENANCE TESTS

Purpose	Factors to consider (in addition to those of Table 2)
1. Establish the "affective status" of the product compared with competition.	Respondents should include regular consumers of the product from all major groups (sex, age, ethnic, income, social) and also a sampling of regular consumers of each of the principal competing products.
2. When "unavoidable" variations occur, as shown by in-house panel tests, establish how these are viewed by the consumers.	As A.1. Attempt to include consumers especially sensitive to the variation in question. By series of tests, attempt to discover which attributes "drive" preference.

B. PRODUCT IMPROVEMENT/OPTIMIZATION STUDIES

1. To test prototypes shown by in-house panel tests to be improvements in what is assumed to be "critical" attributes.	As A.2. Include questions asking the consumer to rate or scale the attributes thought to be critical. Again, a major purpose is to discover which attributes "drive" preference.
2. Optimization: to test series of prototypes in which key attributes or ingredients are varied in a systematic manner.	As B.1. In optimization studies it is necessary that preference be rated on a scale of liking, e.g. 0 = do not like at all, 15 = like extremely. Only two or three attributes can be varied, others should be held constant. Variation should span from "too little" to "too much."

C. DEVELOPMENT OF NEW PRODUCTS

1. Early evaluation of a concept or a prototype.	Focus Group sessions using 10 to 20 target consumers. The choice of panel leader is critical. Focus Groups need to be repeated with several different groups.
2. To compare several early formulations as as to more closely define the new concept.	Product formulation sessions using 10 to 50 target consumers who are taught rating scales for key attributes and then compare several prototypes with the competition. Use scales such as 1 to 15 or line scales so that results can be treated by multivariate statistical methods.
3. To compare more advanced formulations with the competition.	I. Central Location Tests at shopping mall etc. Screen testers as under A.1. The overriding danger here is that subjects, not being used to taste testing, become confused and do not fully understand what is asked of them, or become distracted and give unreliable verdicts.
	II. Home Use Tests. Good screening of subjects (per A.1) is needed. Only two or at most three products can be compared. Safest procedure is monadic (one product one week, second product following week) as subjects will misinterpret any clue in appearance. Only safe question is preference, any scaling question may be misunderstood when no one is there to explain.

| 4. To evaluate competitors as they try to catch up with a successful new product. | Small differences are likely to important. Only in-house panel tests and Home Use Tests are likely to be sensitive enough. |

D. ASSESSMENT OF MARKET POTENTIAL

| 1. To evaluate how much of a new product should be produced and what price can be obtained. | Each of the techniques under C.1 to C.3 are applicable. Critical questions using number scales or line scales are: Intent to purchase, effect of price, effect of convenience features. Effects of advertising may be measured by comparing purchase intent by "exposed" and "non-exposed" subjects." |

E. CATEGORY REVIEW

| 1. To evaluate the position of a brand within its competitive set. To identify areas within a product category where opportunities may exist. | Category review requires descriptive analysis of a broad array of products and/or prototypes that define or cover a category. Typically 20 to 30 products are tested (a) by the in-house descriptive panel and (b) by panels of target consumers. Panels must develop terminology for key attributes or they may use free-choice profiling. Results are evaluated by multivariate analysis techniques. Experience and common sense are needed for evaluation. |

other words, hundreds of compounds exist that affect flavor yet are invisible to the analyst. Indications are that many sulfur compounds and other foul-smelling contaminants are in this group, but also some pleasantly fruity and terpenelike flavors. I think the noble hop aroma is likely to come from such invisible compounds, possibly also a part of the fruity/estery flavor spectrum.

FLAVOR INTENSITY VS. CONCENTRATION

The next step in the research plan was to determine to what degree the threshold of a compound can be used as a measure of its flavor contribution. This called for a complex psychophysical analysis, the results of which can be summarized as shown in Table 4. At 1 Flavor Unit a compound is at its threshold; at 2 FUs the flavor intensity equals twice that amount. This rule, that flavor intensity is directly proportional to concentration, is far from universal; it was found to be strictly valid only in

TABLE 4. Perception of Flavor Differences Expressed in FU (Flavor Units)

FLAVOR INTENSITY: FLAVOR UNITS

FU = concentration/threshold can be used as a rough measure (±20%) for flavor intensity provided (1) the threshold was determined in a type of beer which varies <50% in composition from that studied; (2) the use is limited to the range from 0.2 FU to 2 FU; and (3) the result is taken as a measure of the difference between a test beer and a control beer.

FU can be used as a very rough measure (±50%) in the area 2 to 8 FU and <0.2 FU.

FU cannot be used as a measure (1) of absolute flavor intensity (2) when comparing e.g. beer and cider or beer and 3.6% ethanol.

PERCEPTION OF DIFFERENCES IN FU

A Difference Of:	Is Perceived as:
0-0.5 FU	Not perceptible
0.5-1.0 FU	Perceptible but not identifiable by average taster
1.0-2.0 FU	Detectable and identifiable
Over 2 FU	A complete change of flavor

the narrow area from 0.2 FU to 2.0 FU, and only for comparisons between beers of similar flavor composition. However, this is the area of greatest practical interest. The rule may hold but with considerable variability in the area 2 to 8 FU and below 0.2 FU of flavor difference, and it holds to some degree between dissimilar beers. It does not hold at all for comparison between beer and aqueous alcohol, nor between beer and wine.

FLAVOR INTERACTION

Flavor interaction was studied by adding 26 mixtures of two to six purified compounds to a bland beer and determining the threshold of the mixture together with the flavor type it produced. The results can be summarized as shown in Table 5. Again, these rules are strictly valid only for comparisons between beers of similar flavor composition, and only in the range from 0.2 to 2 FU of added flavor. For example, one can predict that addition of 0.6 FU of acidic flavor from lactic acid plus 0.6 FU of acidic flavor from malic acid will result in 1.2 FU of combined acidic flavor. In two other examples, 0.5 FU of applelike flavor from ethyl hexanoate plus 0.5 FU of bananalike flavor from isoamyl acetate will result in 0.7 FU of combined fruity flavor, while a combination of 0.5 FU of butyric acid with 0.5 FU of diacetyl will produce approximately 0.6 FU of combined rancid butter flavor.

TABLE 5. Flavor Interaction Between Compounds in Beer

GENERAL HYPOTHESIS

1. Substances of like flavors are perceived as additive.

2. Substances with widely different flavors are perceived as independent.

3. Strong synergisms or antagonisms are absent.

4. Typically the combined effect of several flavor compounds amounts to two-thirds of the sum of the components.

THE CHEMIST'S APPROACH

CHEMICAL COMPOSITION OF BEER FLAVOR

The results of model experiments and multi-variate analysis according to Research Plan 3 can be summarized as shown in Table 6. The Table shows the compounds that have been identified in the order from the most flavor active to the least flavor active. It is convenient to divide the 900 or so components into primary, secondary, tertiary and background. Primary flavor components are those present above 2 FU. Removal of a primary component will lead to a drastic change in a product's flavor. A typical American lager has only 3 primary components, isohumulones, ethanol and carbon dioxide. Specialty beers can have many, for example hop-oil derived compounds in hoppy beers, or maltol and other caramel substances in dark beers, or fermentation esters in strong products such as a barley wine or some malt liquors.

TABLE 6. Summary of the Chemical Composition of Beer Flavor

(A) PRIMARY FLAVOR CONSTITUENTS, PRESENT ABOVE 2 FU

Flavor Term	Flavor-Active Compound or Group of Compounds	Typical or Distinctive Member of Group
In typical, Pale Lager Beers:		
1200 Bitter	Hop bitter substanccs	*trans*-isohumulone
0110 Alcoholic	Ethanol	Ethanol
1360 Carbonation	Carbon dioxide	Carbon disoxide
In Specialty Beers:		
0171 Kettle hop	Hop oil transformation products	Oxygenated humulenes
0172 Dry hop	Hop oil constituents	Myrcene, humulene
0410 Caramel	O-heterocyclic ketones	Maltol and isomers
0130 Ester	Esters	3-methylbutyl acetate
1000 Sweet	Sugars	Sucrose

(B) SECONDARY FLAVOR CONSTITUENTS, PRESENT BETWEEN 0.5 AND 2 FU

Compounds Listed Under Specialty Beers above, plus the following:

0131 Isoamyl acetate	Banana esters	3-Methylbutyl acetate, 2-methylpropyl acetate
0132 Ethyl hexanoate	Apple esters	Ethyl hexanoate, ethyl octanoate
0110 Alcoholic	Fusel alcohols	3-Methylbutanol
0732 DMS	Dialkyl sulfides	Dimethyl sulfide
0611 Caprylic	C-6 to C-12 fatty acids	Octanoic acid
0910 Acetic	Acetic and propanoic acids	Acetic acid
0133 Ethyl acetate	Ethyl acetate	Ethyl acetate
0620 Diacetyl	Vicinal diketones	Diacetyl
0613 Isovaleric	3-Methylbutanoic and 1-pentanoic acids	3-Methylbutanoic acid
0612 Butyric	Butanoic and 2-methylpropanoic acids	Butanoic acid
0920 Sour	Other organic acids	Citric, malic acids
1340 Astringent	Polyphenols	Leucocyanidin
1000 Sweet	Sugars	Maltotriose
1410 Body and other terms	Amino acids, small peptides, nucleic acid derivatives	Proline

(C) TERTIARY FLAVOR CONSTITUENTS, PRESENT BETWEEN 0.1 AND 0.5 FU

Numerous Compounds, such as the following:

0140 Fruity	Lactones of hydroxy acids	*gamma*-decalactone
0161 2-Phenylethanol	2-Phenylethanol	2-Phenylethanol
0820 Papery	Long-chain aliphatic aldehydes	*trans*-2-nonenal
0500 Phenolic	Volatile phenols	4-vinalguaiacol
0721 H_2S	Hydrogen sulfide	Hydrogen sulfide
0724 Lightstruck	3-Methyl-2-butene thiol, other thiols	3-Methyl-2-butene thiol
1100 Salty	Inorganic salts	Sodium chloride
1330 Metallic	Metal ions	Ferrous ion

Background Flavor Constituents, Present below 0.1 FU
All Other Flavor Constituents (Probably Thousands)

Secondary flavor components are those present between 0.5 FU and 2 FU. Removal of a secondary component only leads to a minor change in flavor. However, taken together the secondary components probably make up the major part of a beer's flavor impact. In the order of flavor activity one often finds the hop aroma compounds first. Then perhaps the maltol and other caramel compounds, especially in dark beers. In a pale beer of low hop rate the various fermentation esters would come first. Among the fermentation esters we find the banana esters which are the acetates of the fusel alcohols, and the apple esters which are the ethyl esters of butyric, caproic, caprylic, and capric acids. In a group of its own we find ethyl acetate which has a light, solventlike flavor.

To our surprise we found that the various fusel alcohols had warm and pleasantly alcoholic flavors. The unpleasant fusel-oil flavor found in raw distilled products are probably carbonyl compounds formed during the distillation.

Alkyl sulfides like dimethyl sulfide have the flavor of cooked sweet corn. They come from precursors in malt dried at low temperatures and they accumulate if a brew is kept a long time in the hot wort receiver. The caprylic acids are formed by the yeast and they smell faintly goatlike. As surprising as it may sound, these are one main reason that beer is beery: they are pleasant in small amounts, and they are not flavor active in wine or liquor.

Other secondary flavor components include isovaleric acid which comes from hops and is cheesy, the lower fatty acids which taste of vinegar, and diacetyl and butyric acid which have milky/buttery flavors. Next come citric, malic and lactic acids with a clean acid flavor, plus polyphenols, higher sugars and peptides. Nearly all of the secondary components rise to become primary in at least some specialty beers. In addition to those I mentioned, we can find the cheesy flavors in England in some Draft Bitter ales made with aged hops, and the vinegary acids abound in Lambic and Gueze. Pilsner Urquell is an example of a beer high in polyphenols, and many nonalcoholic beers are high in sugars and peptides.

The tertiary flavor components are those ranging from 0.1 to 0.5 FU. Removal of one of these would not cause any perceptible change in overall flavor, but taken together the tertiary components are responsible for many flavor notes. Lactones and phenylethanol, for example, give fruity/alcoholic notes. Long-chain aldehyde like 2-nonenal are the main cause of stale cardboard flavor. Other tertiary components are acetaldehyde, volatile phenols, hydrogen sulfide, mercaptans, inorganic salts, metal ions, stale-flavor esters, and many others. Any one of these groups can give rise to off-flavors when present in too high concentration.

Finally there are the more than 700 components listed here as background, under 0.1 FU. One can speculate what contribution they make. Probably at least some: 100 compounds each at 0.1 FU using the two-thirds rule should contribute 6.7 FU. My guess from looking over the list of background components is that they contribute less than 20 percent of the total.

WHICH FLAVOR TERMS CAN BE EXPLAINED?

Using the known thresholds and flavor interactions, we can calculate or estimate a number of flavor notes on the basis of chemical analysis. Table 7 is a status list of beer flavor research. It shows forty-three common terms out of the 122. Of these

TABLE 7. Degree to Which Various Flavor Notes
Can Be Explained as Arising from Specific Constituents

Can Be Calculated	Can be Partly Explained	Cannot Be Explained
0110 Alcoholic	0120 Solventlike	0111 Spicy
0143 Banana	0144 Blackcurrant	0112 Vinous
0130 Estery	0170 Hoppy	0122 Can-liner
0150 Acetaldehyde	0320 Malty	0163 Perfumy
0611 Caprylic	0330 Worty	0210 Resinous
0612 Cheesy	0410 Caramel	0211 Woody
0614 Butyric	0423 Smoky	0230 Grassy
0620 Diacetyl	0503 Carbolic	0310 Grainy
0710 Sulfitic	0630 Rancid	0740 Yeasty
0721 H_2S	0700 Sulfury	
0732 DMS	0720 Sulfidic	
0910 Acetic	0810 Catty	
1200 Bitter	0820 Papery	
1330 Metallic	0840 Moldy	
1360 Carbonation	0920 Sour	
	1000 Sweet	
	1100 Salty	
	1370 Warming	
	1411 Watery	
	1413 Satiating	

forty-three, there are fifteen flavor notes for which we can calculate or estimate the strength. There are eighteen we can partly explain, and then 100 that we cannot at present explain, though we may have some promising hypotheses.

LIMITATIONS OF THE ABOVE RULES

The rules for calculating flavor impact that I have proposed must not be taken for more than they are. The formulas will be useful for someone working with a single flavor element. For example, if a beer suffers from a diacetyl off-flavor, then it is reasonable to assume that if the concentration of diacetyl and pentanedione can be reduced, then the problem will go away. But flavor calculations become inaccurate if any more complicated change is made, such as a change of yeast. For anything complex, the way out is to do careful tasting with

TABLE 8. The Author's List of Desirable and Undesirable Flavor Notes in Beer

Desirable	Desirable in Small Amounts	Desirable in Specialty Beers	Indifferent Unless in Excess	Undesirable
Bitter	Caprylic	Honey	Other ester	Moldy
Alcoholic	DMS	Licorice	Roses	Metallic
Carbonation	H$_2$S	Cheesy	Other flower	Worty
Noble-hop	Mercaptan	Cloverlike	Perfumy	Grainy
Dry-hop	Diacetyl	Other spice	Resinous	Strawlike
Malty	Sweet	Woodruff	Yeasty	Woody
Caramel	Salty	Other herb	Acetaldehyde	Bready
Astringent	Sour	Cherry	Sulfitic	Papery
Banana ester	Warming	Other fruit	Grassy	Chlorophenol
Apple ester	Cooling	Acetic	Burnt	Rancid
Acidic	Vinous	Phenolic		Oily
Body	Nutty	Smoky		Skunky
				Catty
				Stale

many well-trained panelists and many repeats. In general, if the gas chromatograph and the panel disagree, one should trust the panel and not the machine. There are quite a few other limitations, for example with regard to how many different flavor notes a person can cope with. Sometimes the panel can taste a difference but no one can say in what part of the flavor spectrum the difference lies. I'll skip these and instead try to define which are the desirable flavor elements in a beer.

DEFINING THE FLAVOR ELEMENTS

DESIRABLE AND UNDESIRABLE FLAVOR ELEMENTS

What follows is my own subjective opinion, not an outcome of objective tests. Table 8 is my list of desirables and undesirables. The building blocks of all beers are in the first column. These are of course bitterness, alcoholic flavor, and carbonation. Beers without maltiness and caramel flavor exist but they are rare. Beers without alcoholic flavor are not so rare these days. Without at least some astringency, some fermentation esters, and some acidity and body, a beer is unlikely to be saleable. How anyone conceived the idea of beers without at least some hop character I do not understand. To me such beers are like an omelette without eggs.

The notes in the second column are desirable in small amounts. Without a little DMS, a little diacetyl, sweetness, etc., a beer is bland and uninviting. Those in the third column are specific spicy, herblike or other notes used in specialty beers. Together, the flavor elements in the second and third columns are what marks the difference between good beers and great beers, just as a very similar list could be made to mark the difference between good cooking and great cooking.

The fourth column contains flavor elements that are indifferent, e.g. flowery, resinous, sulfury, burnt. These occur as byproducts and are not unpleasant unless in excess. Finally the fifth column contains flavor defects like moldy, metallic, oily or stale that are undesirable in any amount. I will not spend time on those except to say that many a microbrewer has lost his shirt by trying to sell (and not destroy) a beer that was "off" in this direction. As for the larger brewers, I think it ranks as an All-American scandal that fully half of all the interesting and unusual packaged beers that are on the market, get to us so oxidized that staleness and cardboard are the main flavor notes.

FLAVOR COMPOSITION OF THE WORLDS' BEERS

Here is where we start putting the flavors together again. Figure 1 shows the principal elements according to strength in fresh beers from around the world. Inherent in the approach is the assumption that the senses of smell and taste are "analytical" like pitch discrimination and not "synthetic" like color vision. If indeed we perceive flavor as we hear an orchestra, then these are the major instruments. A typical North American lager has 1 to 2 FU of sweetness and acidity, and 2 to 3 FU of bitterness. In Mexico the range is 2 to 4 FU of bitterness. In hop character the North American lager can vary from 0.5 to about 3 FU. Alcoholic flavor in North American lager runs at 2 to 3 FU and so does fruity/estery, caramelized flavor around 1 FU, DMS always below 1 FU, and carbonation as a rule is high at about 3 FU.

The beers that run up to 10 FU in bitterness and hop character are of course the central European Pilsen types. Pilsner Urquell is high in both and also in malty character and in astringency from hop and malt tannins, but it is low in fruity/estery character and in carbonation. Koenig Pils, Jever and Bitburg are German pilsners which emphasize bitterness over hop character. The beers that go to 100 FU of caramel flavor are the stouts like Guinness and Mackeson. Those high in alcoholic and estery flavors are of course the strong beers like malt liquors and barley wines from the United Kingdom, and those German beers with names ending in -ator. Brown and Clapperton found by multivariate analysis that ales can be differentiated from lagers by being low in DMS and high in caramel, whereas lagers are high in DMS and low in caramel flavor.

Examples of acidic beers are Berliner Weisse and above all the Lambic beers of Brussels; both types owe their flavor to lactic acid bacteria, as do yogurts. Many great beers which emphasize yeast flavor have a hint of the caprylic; beer wouldn't be "beery" without caprylicness, as mentioned. Some examples are in Mexico. Central European lagers emphasize DMS; examples are Grolsch from Holland and most German Helles and Märzen beers. A mite of diacetyl is found in many British lagers, and you can find quite perceptible cheesy flavors in some of their hoppy ales for which the Golding hops are deliberately kept at room temperature for over a year. A famous beer type with a pronounced phenolic and clovelike flavor is the Bavarian Weizenbier.

HISTORY OF BEER FLAVOR

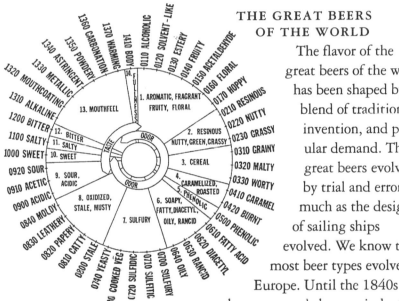

THE GREAT BEERS OF THE WORLD

The flavor of the great beers of the world has been shaped by a blend of tradition, invention, and popular demand. The great beers evolved by trial and error, much as the design of sailing ships evolved. We know that most beer types evolved in Europe. Until the 1840s beer was made by non-industrial procedures and no one expected it to keep beyond two weeks nor to travel beyond thirty miles or so, but the industrial and scientific revolution slowly changed that. It had long been known that strong and heavily hopped beers were much more resistant to souring. Now Czech and German brewers found that if these hoppy brews were bottom fermented and cold stored, the beer could stay haze free. So suddenly it became possible for an

FIGURE 1. Principal flavor elements in fresh beers from around the world.

industrious tavern keeper to offer beers from further away. In 1842 the merchants in Pilsen pooled their capital and built what was to remain the world's largest brewery for forty years, or well into the 1880s. They took advantage of the vast underground caves they could excavate under Pilsen where the temperature was low and even. By 1860 they were shipping Urquell not only throughout the Austro-Hungarian Empire but over much of central Europe.

A tavern or restaurant owner who wanted to provide something better or even just something different from the local brew had little choice other than the large Bohemian brands like Urquell and Budweiser, who could charge whatever the traffic would bear. Beginning in the 1860s the rootlouse phylloxera destroyed the vineyards, so the consumer who wanted the best likewise had no choice but to pay and to learn to like very bitter and hoppy beers. People always knew that many of the satisfying things in life are acquired tastes; examples are oysters and steak tartare, sushi and spirits. Competition to the Bohemians for a long time was restricted to a smaller scale by the need to build ice storage, but by the 1870s ice machines such as Linde's ammonia compressor made it possible for any brewer to expand if he had the product and the capital.

Those best placed to challenge Pilsen's monopoly were the Bavarians, and it was companies like Spaten and Löwenbräu who were the ones to take away Pilsen's lead. They were able to provide adequate microbiological stability at 30 BU rather than 40. The Munich beers also were brewed with a proportion of Munich malt which gave a higher color, more mellow aroma and better flavor stability than Pilsen's. Next, Vienna began to export an even milder and darker beer, then Dortmund joined the fray with a pale but strong beer, also less bitter.

Meanwhile in England people did not adopt the cold fermentation solution. Whitbread invited Pasteur who helped them get rid of the bacteria by acid-washing the yeast and by aseptic techniques. The British solved the haze problem without a need for cooling, by inventing clarification with isinglass from fish bladders collected off Malaya. Their biggest remaining problem was premature yeast flocculation, which they resolved with miraculous contraptions like the Burton Union system. The system by the way makes the most wonderful Pale Ale and Best Bitter.

Finally in Ireland the Guinness solution was to make a beer at 50 BU, so bitter that no bacterium could grow, so dark that even the yeast need not be removed. By the gay 1890s these and hundreds of other types were competing across Europe and the Americas. Technology became available to everyone, and the scene changed slowly to one of competitions, where brewers were furiously perfecting their types.

The 1890s and early 1900s were the decades of the café society and a great time for beer lovers. From London to Vienna and from Moscow to San Francisco people sharpened their taste buds and joined the satisfying hunt for good beer. Like the real ales in England today, sometimes products were cloudy, sometimes sour, even acetic, even viscous or "ropy," but when they were good, they were superb. And as much as in the taste, "the pleasure was in the hunt, the gaining of experience, the pursuit of the elusive, the possibility of triumph or disaster."

The early 1900s were also the heyday of the brewing consultant. He would arrive in a Rolls Royce, dressed in coat and tails. He would ceremoniously taste the beer, then pronounce his recommendation, and charge an enormous fee. He knew the more he could charge, the more likely was the brewer to follow his advice. One North American adherent to this philosophy was Frank Schwaiger of Anheuser-Busch. He looked with disdain at taste panels and consumer tests; what you need, he said, was one person with "Bierverstand," or "intuitive beer knowledge." This was in the days when brewers aimed at perfecting one product per company. He was right for his time and company, the product he perfected was one that his marketing department could indeed sell, but he might have a difficult time today, when the accent is on developing a product for every nook and cranny of the market.

DESIGNER BEERS

I'll jump now from traditional European brewing right to today's craze for what Michael Jackson calls designer beers. Young people today, as you know, would not be seen dead with any ordinary mass-produced beer on their table or even in their refrigerator. Demand grows every day for beers that make a statement about the drinker's product knowledge and his or her feel for fashion. Some brewers complain of having to brew and package many products. I think such a brewer is seriously misinformed: we should be overjoyed. What we see is that the best of our consumers delight in acquiring product knowledge and in sharing it with their friends. They are treating beer the way a connoisseur talks about wine, the way a gourmet enjoys food. They drink to enjoy, not to intoxicate. They may drink less, but they do not object to spending more per beer. What better customers can a brewer have?

The brewer today has the technical possibilities of emphasizing or deemphasizing almost any one of the individual flavor elements in Tables 6 to 8. In Table 9, I have collected some of the properties the brewer can use to increase the perceived value of a beer. Some examples: dry beers were successful in Tokyo because they set out to combine the properties high alcohol, unpasteurized, dry, macho, and "with it," and were heavily advertised. In flavor they were nothing special, just more alcoholic and less bitter. Their United States counterparts ran into our neo-prohibitionism and could not be high in alcohol, so one at least chose instead to make a virtue of there being little flavor and emphasize "no aftertaste."

TABLE 9. Properties the Brewer Can Use to Increase the Perceived Value of a Beer

Special Technical Properties	Special Flavor Properties	Image Characteristics
High alcohol	Freshness	Imported
Low alcohol	Dryness	Costly to make
No Alcohol	Noble hop	Advertised
Low calorie	Low bitter	Gourmet
Unpasteurized	Flavor stable	Macho, strong
Long storage	No aftertaste	Refined, elegant
No additives	Fancy flavors	Traditional
Convenience	Lime, citrus	With it
Pure water	Beery, cool	Curiosity
All malt	Smoky	Fun, good cheer

A second example is the no-alcohol beers: the potential demand is there, but brewers struggle with the worty, grainy or strawlike flavors and with finding a substitute for the flavor of alcohol itself. A third example: the importers as you know have had great and growing success with traditional specialty brews from old Europe, from sour Belgian Gueze to fresh and gassy Berliner Weisse, to smoky Bamberg Rauchbier to alcoholic Bavarian Salvator. Likewise the local mini- and microbrewers have had success by showing inventiveness and enterprise. Like a good cook, they try to brew something their customers will really like. They are not trying to brew more cheaply, or more fault-free. They are trying to brew a beer people will like, one people will talk about, one people will discuss with their friends. My feeling is that there is great scope for brewers today, with luck many, many more both small and large brewers will be successful with designer beers.

Reprinted with permission from **MBAA Technical Quarterly**, *Vol. 28, 1991, pp. 132-40.*

SENSORY ASPECTS OF ZYMOLOGICAL EVALUATION

DAVID W. EBY, PH.D.

The interest in having homebrew evaluated has increased dramatically over the last several years. Commercially, the evaluation of beer has become an important advertising boon. The Boston Beer Company has built an advertising program on the claim that their Samuel Adams Lager was voted "the winner of the Great American Beer Festival for three years in a row." This claim is based on the fact that Samuel Adams was voted best beer in a consumer preference poll at the 1989, 1990 and 1991 Great American Beer Festivals (a national competition for commercial breweries). With so much interest, emphasis and capital placed on the outcome of zymological competitions, it is important to understand the task of the evaluator.

Many factors are involved in being a good judge, including training, experience, and understanding of the brewing process. For these reasons the AHA and Home Wine and Beer Trade Association organized the Beer Judge Certification Program (BJCP) to provide training, set standards, give experience in judging and evaluating the judges themselves for competence and experience. I think that equal importance should be placed on understanding of the psychological aspects of the evaluation process.

When tasting a beer, a person is having a psychological experience that is primarily perceptual in nature, but other psychological factors (such as mood) can affect the experience. (Sensations like taste and sight are considered to be psychological, just like emotions and thoughts.) This chapter intends to educate homebrewers about how their sensory systems are used when tasting beers (or other things) and will analyze the factors that can affect a sensory judgment. It is my hope that this information will enhance the quality, consistency and efficiency of judging.

We acquire information about the world through our sensory systems in a process known as perception. A common misconception about perception is that we have only five senses: seeing (vision), hearing (audition), touching (tactile), tasting (gustation) and smelling (olfaction). Sensory psychologists add several more including flavor perception, a combination of taste, touch, smell, and perhaps, vision. When evaluating a beer, a judge uses all of these senses to gauge various characteristics, but certain senses have a strong influence while others contribute minimally.

Another common misconception about perception is that we perceive exactly what is out there in the world (or in a beer), but this is not always the case. For example, a full moon appears bigger on the horizon than when it is overhead. This is a perceptual illusion because the size of the moon is not changing, only your perception of its size. In terms of beer, perception is affected by factors not related to the beer itself. The same beer can be perceived differently depending on many factors, several of which I will discuss below.

Following is a description of the senses and their relation to zymological evaluation, including a discussion of some of the factors that can affect a perceptual judgment, and hence, the score a judge might give a beer.

SEEING

While visual perception is arguably the most important sense in everyday perception, it is of lesser importance in beer evaluation. Vision is used to determine the fill level, amount of sediment in the bottle and assess the head density and thickness, clarity and color of the beer. The scoring system used at AHA-sanctioned events (see page 54) allocates six points (of a fifty-point scale) to the beer's appearance. Thus, 12 percent of the possible points are judged using vision.

A person with normal vision should have little difficulty in evaluating a beer's appearance. No psychological factors are known to affect the accuracy or consistency or appearance judgments, with one notable exception. The perceived color of a beer can be influenced by a number of factors.

Vision operates when the eye is stimulated with light of certain wavelengths. Combinations of different wavelengths roughly correspond to different perceived colors. When light composed of many wavelengths (such as sunlight) passes through a bottle or mug of beer, most of the wavelengths are filtered out — only a few reach the eye. A person looking at the beer from the opposite side of the light source will see only those wavelengths passing through and will perceive the color that corresponds to the particular combination of unfiltered wavelengths. Different types of beers and colored glass filter out different combinations of wavelengths and thus have different colors. (Stouts filter out all wavelengths and appear black or without color).

Moreover, the perceived color, to some degree, is a function of the light source passing through the beer. Consider what happens if you start with a light source that contains only some wavelengths (such as colored light, the light from a standard incandescent bulb or candlelight). The combination of wavelengths that passes through the beer will be different from what is seen when the light source contains all wavelengths. To obtain the most consistent perception of color, judge a beer using a light source that contains all (or a large proportion) of the wavelengths that the eye can sense. Good light sources are sunlight, fluorescent lights and high-pressure xenon lamps.

Another relevant aspect of color perception is something known as the contrast effect. Visual perception of an object varies as a function of what is located near the object. Figure 1 shows the contrast effect. All four beer bottles are the same shade of gray while the surrounding squares are drawn with different gray shades from light to dark. The brightness of the bottles appears different depending on the shade of the surrounding patch. The beer appears darker when judged against a light background than when judged against a dark background. In actual judging, the contrast effect means the background a beer is judged against can alter perception of the color. For example, a light red background might make an amber beer appear dark red, or a green background might give an

Illustration by John Martin

FIGURE 1: An example of the contrast effect. The beer bottles are all drawn with the same gray shade while the background squares are drawn with different gray shades. Notice how the perception of the shade of the beer bottle differs depending on the shade of the background.

amber beer a non-red tint. To obtain consistent judgments of a beer's color, it is best to use a uniform background, preferably a piece of white paper.

HEARING

Next to vision, audition probably is the most important sense for humans but it plays almost no role in zymological evaluation. The only information you can obtain through audition is a general impression of the carbonation level when first opened. If no hiss is heard (an event that has saddened the hearts of many beginning homebrewers), you can conclude the beer is flat. Louder and higher pitched hisses indicate more carbonation. But this information is questionable in zymological evaluation because the carbonation level can be detected in other ways. The one way that auditory information can lead to inconsistent judging could be when one judge opens the bottle while the others are not listening.

TOUCH

The sense of touch mainly involves the skin, including the lips, mouth and tongue. Tactile perception is surprisingly important in zymological evaluation, providing two primary types of information: temperature and pressure (or texture). Because the viscosity (texture) and the rate of release of carbonation are affected by the temperature, it is important to chill beers properly for the style. The AHA scoring system allocates five points for body and nineteen points for flavor, so nearly half of the total points are for the sense of touch.

This sense works by applying pressure to the skin that stimulates nerve cells located there. Because certain areas of skin have a high concentration of nerve cells, some parts of the skin are better at detecting pressure than others. Fortunately for zymological evaluators, the lips and tongue are among the most sensitive parts. The tongue and jaw push the liquid against the roof of the mouth and teeth, creating pressure that stimulates the touch nerve cells. Full-bodied beers create more pressure than do light or medium-bodied beers. You may have heard someone make the comment, "Guinness stout is so thick you have to chew it." Such a comment implies it is possible to discriminate among the bodies of beers solely on the basis of touch.

This ability can be affected because the sense of touch exhibits something known as rapid adaptation. Prolonged pressure on a certain part of the skin will make that part unable to signal it is being pressed on. For example, if you were to rest your arm on a table top, you would initially be aware of the pressure but after a couple of seconds you would no longer feel the table top unless you move your arm. This adaptation occurs in all of the body's skin, including the mouth, lips and tongue. Therefore, zymological evaluators should make sure they judge the body of the beer soon after they sip the beer. Otherwise their ability to make this judgment will rapidly decrease unless they take another sip.

In addition, the inside of the mouth is about 98.6 degrees F. Physicists tell us the viscosity or body of the beer and the rate of carbon dioxide release are directly related to the liquid's temperature. Increases in temperature will lighten the body and increase the rate of carbonation release in the mouth, so the longer the beer remains in the mouth, the higher its temperature will become and the more difficult an accurate judgment of body will be.

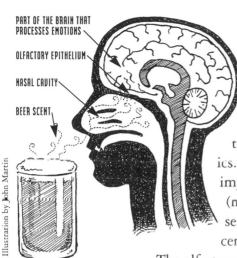

PART OF THE BRAIN THAT
PROCESSES EMOTIONS

OLFACTORY EPITHELIUM

NASAL CAVITY

BEER SCENT

Illustration by John Martin

FIGURE 2: Cut-away view of a typical beer drinker showing the nasal cavity and the various parts of the brain. The molecules from the beer diffuse into the air and are sniffed into the nasal cavity where they pass by the olfactory epithelium. Here they diffuse into the mucus layer covering the olfactory epithelium and are detected by specialized cells. Located directly above the olfactory epithelium is a part of the brain that is known to process emotions and memories.

SMELL

As most of us who enjoy a fine beer know, an important part of the enjoyment is the smell or aroma. In fact, the AHA scoring system allocates ten points or 20 percent to aromatics. Because a beer's aroma is an important component of its flavor (nineteen points), the olfactory sense is involved in about 60 percent of the total score.

The olfactory sense provides information about the chemical composition of the beer, the relative levels of certain chemicals and the presence (or absence) of additives and contaminants. In addition, the scent will often recall emotional responses and even memories of past events. For example, whenever I smell peach lambic, I invariably think back to my wedding reception when, instead of drinking Champagne, my wife and I toasted with peach lambic. A beer that evokes positive emotions and memories by virtue of its distinct smell may be judged more favorably than a beer that provokes negative recollections.

Because the olfactory sense detects chemicals (molecules) that are diffused into the air, it is known as a chemical sense. As shown in Figure 2, the area where the chemical components of beer are detected is hidden in the top, back portion of the nasal cavity at an area called the olfactory epithelium. During a sniff, only about 10 percent of the inhaled air reaches the olfactory epithelium. Research has shown that the judged intensity of a scent is not increased if one sniffs harder to get more air into the nasal cavity. This probably results from the fact that the extra air simply moves into the lungs. On the other hand, a normal breath does not create enough turbulence to get any air into the back of the nasal cavity. Therefore, to get the beer's chemicals to the olfactory epithelium, it is important to sniff, but vigorous sniffs are not necessary.

Located directly above, and many think connected to, the olfactory epithelium is the area of the brain that is known to process emotional responses and certain memories. This connection between the area for smell and the brain probably accounts for the emotional responses and memory flashes associated with certain distinct smells.

The olfactory epithelium contains a layer of cells that are sensitive to various molecules. Surprisingly, these cells are covered with a layer of mucus (the substance that normally coats the inside of your nose and increases in quantity when you get a cold). Chemicals must pass through this mucus to get to the cells of the olfactory epithelium and be detected.

Four main factors can affect the ability to efficiently perceive the aroma of beer. First, changes in the thickness of the mucus layer will change the amount of molecules that make it through the mucus to the olfactory epithelium. As you have probably noticed, having a cold can reduce your sense of smell because clogged nasal passages do not allow air to enter the nasal cavity, and also because the mucus layer over the olfactory epithelium is thickened. Smoking, eating spicy foods (horseradish), using nasal sprays (of the type used for colds) and taking certain drugs (antibiotics, cocaine) can affect the thickness of this layer. Judges who believe their olfactory ability is reduced for whatever reason should voluntarily refrain from judging a competition until their sense of smell returns. Furthermore, to prevent diminished olfactory ability, it is best to prevent cigarette smoke from wafting around the judges during a competition.

A second factor influencing the sense of smell is the state of the cells in the olfactory epithelium. Certain fumes (like those from paint and ammonia), smoke and nasally-ingested drugs can damage these cells so they cannot respond to scent chemicals. Following such damage it can take up to three weeks for the cells to be replaced (in some cases they are never replaced), knocking out the sense of smell in the meantime.

The third factor is simply individual variations in olfactory ability. Some people have a superb sense of smell and are able to detect a wide range of chemicals in very small quantities. In general, this ability is best for women and decreases with age. However, many older people have excellent olfactory abilities.

The fourth factor influencing smell perception is that olfaction shows rapid adaptation, similar to what we discussed for touch perception. This means that an initial perception of a strong odor will quickly decrease in perceived intensity until it is no longer detectable. You can experience this by conducting the following demonstration. Get a strong odorant like nail polish, ammonia or an onion and place it next to you while you read the rest of the this chapter. In about ten minutes, you will probably notice the smell has dramatically decreased in intensity, if you can even smell it anymore. As with touch, beer evaluators should make their judgment of aroma as soon as possible after the first sniff. Otherwise, their sensitivity to the chemicals in the beer will rapidly diminish as will the ability to effectively evaluate the aroma.

TASTE

Gustatory, or taste, perception probably is the most heralded sense in the culinary arts (such as beermaking). It is this sense that most people believe forms the foundation for zymological evaluation. As we already mentioned, the AHA scoring system allocated nineteen points to the beer's flavor. However, taste and flavor perception are not the same thing. A beer's flavor is greatly influenced by its taste, but is also affected by its smell, feel and probably even its appearance. Therefore, based on the AHA scoring system, the information obtained from the gustatory sense is involved in somewhere around 30 percent of the total score.

Gustatory perception is similar to olfaction in that it is a chemical sense. The gustatory sense, however, detects chemicals dissolved in a solution rather than diffused in the air. It allows a person to determine the basic chemical composition of substances in the mouth.

The taste sensations can be divided into four categories: sweet, salty, sour and bitter. Many sensory psychologists believe all tastes are a combination of these four basic units. The organ of taste is, of course, the tongue. Located on the tongue are a bunch of cells called taste buds. (The name is derived from their rosebud appearance rather than their ability to detect a certain domestic beer!) These cells seem to be arranged so that groups of taste buds signal a certain basic taste sensation.

Sensory psychologists have mapped the locations of these groups on the tongue (Figure 3). The area that senses sweet is on the tip. To perceive the sweet quality of a substance, you must place that substance on the tip of the tongue. If something is placed only on the tip of the tongue you will not be able to taste sour or bitter characteristics. You can test this with a simple demonstration. Carefully place a drop of lemon juice on the tip of your tongue. While your tongue is sticking out of your mouth, close your eyes and determine if you can taste the sourness. (This part must be done with the tongue out of your mouth. If you close your mouth the juice will quickly coat your tongue. I recommend doing this demonstration in the privacy of your own home!) Now pull the tongue back in and close your mouth, allowing the lemon juice to move to the sides of the tongue where you will likely taste the sour characteristics.

The taste bud map has several consequences for zymological evaluation. If you have never seen beer being evaluated (or have never judged a competition yourself), you may be unaware that beer judges swallow their sips of beer. This would be a major breach of etiquette during a wine tasting competition. However, there is a good reason why beer judges swallow in order to evaluate a beer's taste. Unlike wine, one of the most important taste characteristics of a beer is bitterness. As shown in Figure 3, the taste buds that signal bitterness are located far back and partly down the throat. To detect the bittering hops the beer must pass over these taste buds and by the time these taste buds are stimulated, the beer is well on its way down your throat. This is why the aftertaste often consists of the bitter characteristics. I jokingly tell perception students that because a beer's taste is a combination

Illustration by John Martin

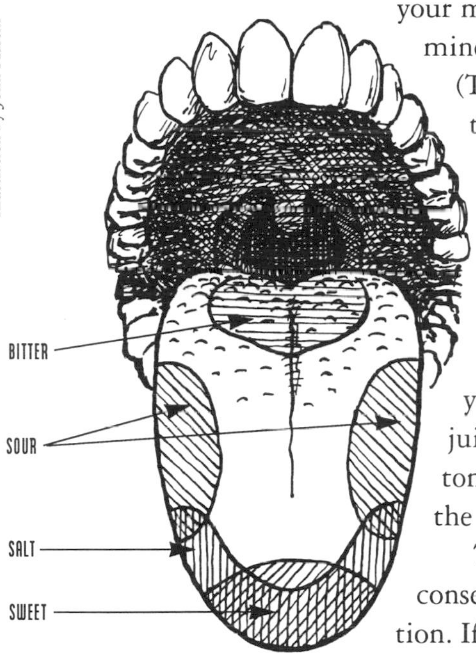

BITTER
SOUR
SALT
SWEET

FIGURE 3: A schematic depiction of a tongue. The labeled regions show areas where taste buds that detect chemicals associated with certain tastes are clustered. These locations are only approximate and, undoubtedly, vary slightly from person to person.

of all four of the the basic taste categories and a wine's taste is only a combination of three, the argument can be made that a beer drinker's palate is more sophisticated than a wine drinkers!

As in gustatory perception, the ability to sense different tastes can be influenced by several factors. The two most important are damage to the taste buds and interference of tasting abilities caused by the presence of other chemicals in the mouth. The taste buds have a lifespan of about ten days and are continually dying and being replaced. Fortunately some taste buds are being replaced while others are dying, so there are always live taste buds ready to detect chemicals. However, a large number of taste buds in a localized area of the tongue can be simultaneously damaged causing a loss of tasting ability in that area until they have been replaced. This type of damage most frequently occurs when you eat food that is too hot. The heat may wipe out a whole area of taste buds, requiring several days to be replaced and diminishing a person's ability to perceive bitterness, sweetness, saltiness or sourness (depending on the injured area). Other events that can prematurely destroy taste buds (and temporarily alter tasting abilities) are smoking, eating spicy or acidic food (fresh pineapple) and using certain chemicals (some mouthwashes).

The residual chemicals that remain in the mouth after a beer is sampled can also affect taste perception. To prevent this from happening many judges eat crackers or some other food to "clear their palate." However, this introduces different chemicals into the mouth that could affect later taste perception (and judging scores), especially if the food has a high salt or sugar content. To minimize this problem, wine evaluators eat unleavened and unsalted crackers. Another way to remove many of the residual chemicals in the mouth is to rinse with a neutral liquid, such as water at room temperature. Some chemicals, however, cannot be easily removed. You may have noticed this if you have brushed your teeth right before going down to your favorite brewpub.

FLAVOR

I have saved flavor perception for last because it is the product of combining the information gathered from smell, taste and touch (and possibly vision). I distinguish flavor perception from other perceptions because, when a substance is placed in the mouth, it has a smell, texture and taste. Alterations in any of these sensations will affect the flavor of the substance. It is perhaps easier to understand what I mean by trying another demonstration that, again, you will probably want to try in the privacy of your own home. Place a small piece of apple and piece of potato of equal size on a plate in front of you. Close your eyes and spin the plate several times so that you do not know which piece is which. Pinch your nostrils shut and place one of the pieces in your mouth. Try to guess which piece you are chewing. Most likely you will have a difficult time making this judgment. By pinching your nostrils you have removed the olfactory information that contributes partly to the flavor of foods.

The AHA scoring system has a category title flavor worth a total of nineteen points. In the AHA system, the term flavor is used in a different way than it is used here. The AHA system includes gustatory (taste) and flavor information in this category, with no designation as to the relative contributions of each type of information. According to my definition, flavor is the perception that results from the combined information from the other senses. Thus flavor perception merits a separate judgment category right beside that for taste perception. Regardless of this difference, because the perceived flavor is affected by the perceived smell, texture, taste and appearance of the beer, flavor perception may be involved in as much as forty of the fifty points in the AHA judging scale.

Because the flavor of beer is a combination of all the sensory information, any of the factors that influence a certain sense (like smell) also will influence the perceived flavor. For example, a judge who has a temporarily deficient olfactory sense could exhibit inconsistencies not only in the aroma category (ten points), but also in the flavor category (nineteen points). This could result in inefficient judging for twenty-nine of the fifty points used in evaluating a beer.

CONCLUSION

We have reviewed the basic perceptual systems used by a zymological evaluator when judging beer and some of the factors that can affect the performance of these systems. You may have noted that in this entire discussion we did not talk about any factors that change the physical characteristics of the beer; the discussion was limited to the factors that affect the perceived components of beer. Thus, you should be aware that the perceived characteristics of any given beer can vary greatly depending upon the factors discussed in this article, even when the physical characteristics of the beer have not changed.

The drinking or evaluation of beer is a sensory process. By having a thorough understanding of how each sense acquires information, zymological evaluators and all people who enjoy quality beer should be able to increase their consistency and accuracy in judging competitions as well as increase their enjoyment of drinking beer.

American Homebrewers Association
1993 Beer Score Sheet

The following is the 1993 American Homebrewers Association's beer score sheet. The score sheet is updated annually and used in homebrew competitions. For more information on the National Homebrew Competition, Beer Judge Certification Program or Sanctioned Competition Program, call or write the American Homebrewers Association, PO Box 1679, Boulder, CO, 80306-1679, (303) 447-0816, FAX (303) 447-2825.

DESCRIPTOR DEFINITIONS
✔ **CHECK WHENEVER APPROPRIATE**

☐ **Acetaldehyde** — Green applelike aroma; byproduct of fermentation.

☐ **Alcoholic** — The general effect of ethanol and higher alcohols. Tastes warming.

☐ **Astringent** — Drying, puckering (like chewing on a grape skin) feeling often associated with sourness. Tannin. Most often derived from boiling of grains, long mashes, oversparging or sparging with hard water.

☐ **Bitter** — Basic taste associated with hops; braun-hefe or malt husks. Sensation experienced on back of tongue.

☐ **Chill haze** — Haze caused by precipitation of protein-tannin compound at cold temperatures. Does not affect flavor. Reduction of proteins or tannins in brewing or fermenting will reduce haze.

☐ **Chlorophenolic** — Caused by chemical combination of chlorine and organics. Detectable in parts per billion. Aroma is unique but similar to plasticlike phenolic. Avoid using chlorinated water.

☐ **Cooked Vegetable/Cabbagelike** — Aroma and flavor often due to long lag times and wort spoilage bacteria that later are killed by alcohol produced in fermentation.

☐ **Diacetyl/Buttery** — Described as buttery, butterscotch. Sometimes caused by abbreviated fermentation or bacteria.

☐ **DMS** (dimethyl sulfide) — A sweet, cornlike aroma/flavor. Can be attributed to malt, short or non-vigorous boiling of wort, slow wort chilling or, in extreme cases, bacterial infection.

☐ **Fruity/Estery** — Similar to banana, raspberry, pear, apple or strawberry flavor; may include other fruity/estery flavors. Often accentuated with higher temperature fermentations and certain yeast strains.

☐ **Grainy** — Raw grain flavor. Cereallike. Some amounts are appropriate in some beer styles.

☐ **Hoppy** — Characteristic odor of the essential oil of hops. Does not include hop bitterness.

☐ **Husky** — See Astringent.

☐ **Light-Struck** — Having the characteristic smell of a skunk, caused by exposure to light. Some hops can have a very similar character.

☐ **Metallic** — Caused by exposure to metal. Also described as tinny, coins, bloodlike. Check your brewpot and caps.

☐ **Oxidized/Stale** — Develops in the presence of oxygen as beer ages or is exposed to high temperatures; winy, wet cardboard, papery, rotten vegetable/pineapple, sherry, baby diapers. Often coupled with an increase in sour, harsh and bitter. The more aeration in bottling/siphoning or air in headspace, the more quickly a beer will oxidize. Warm temperatures dramatically accelerate oxidation.

☐ **Phenolic** — Can be any one or combination of a medicinal, plastic, electrical fire, Listerinelike, Band-Aidlike, smoky, clovelike aroma or flavor. Most often caused by wild strains of yeast or bacteria. Can be extracted from grains (see astringent). Sanitizing residues left in equipment can contribute.

☐ **Salty** — Flavor associated with table salt. Sensation experienced on sides of tongue. Can be caused by presence of too much sodium chloride, calcium chloride or magnesium sulfate (Epsom salts); brewing salts.

☐ **Solventlike** — Flavor and aromatic character of certain alcohols, often due to high fermentation temperatures. Like acetone, lacquer thinner.

☐ **Sour/Acidic** — Pungent aroma, sharpness of taste. Basic taste like vinegar or lemon; tart. Typically associated with lactic or acetic acid. Can be the result of bacterial infection through contamination or the use of citric acid. Sensation experienced on sides of tongue.

☐ **Sweet** — Basic taste associated with sugar. Sensation experienced on front tip of tongue.

☐ **Sulfurlike (H$_2$S; Hydrogen sulfide)** — Rotten eggs, burning matches. Is a byproduct with certain strains of yeast. Fermentation temperature can be a factor of intensity. Diminishes with age. Most evident with bottle-conditioned beer.

☐ **Yeasty** — Yeastlike flavor. Often due to strains of yeast in suspension or beer sitting on sediment too long.

American Homebrewers Association
1993 Beer Score Sheet

Round No. _____ **Entry No.** _____

Category No. _____

Subcategory (spell out) _____

Judged By (please print)_____

Judge Qualifications (check one): ☐ Recognized   ☐ Certified

☐ National   ☐ Master   ☐ Experienced (but not in BJCP)

☐ Apprentice or Novice   ☐ Other: _____

BOTTLE INSPECTION Comments _____

_____

		Max. Score
BOUQUET/AROMA (as appropriate for style)	10	_____

Malt (3), Hops (3), Other Aromatic Characteristics (4)

Comments _____

_____

APPEARANCE (as appropriate for style)   6 _____
Color (2), Clarity (2), Head Retention (2)

Comments _____

_____

FLAVOR (as appropriate for style)   19 _____
Malt (3), Hops (3), Conditioning (2), Aftertaste (3), Balance (4), Other Flavor Characteristics (4)

Comments _____

_____

BODY (full or thin as appropriate for style)   5 _____

Comments _____

_____

DRINKABILITY & OVERALL IMPRESSION   10 _____

Comments _____

_____

TOTAL (50 possible points): _____

Scoring Guide		
Excellent (40-50):	Exceptionally exemplifies style, requires little or no attention
Very Good (30-39):	Exemplifies style well, requires some attention
Good (25-29):	Exemplifies style satisfactorily, but requires attention
Drinkable (20-24):	Does not exemplify style, requires attention
Problem (<20):	Problematic, requires much attention NHC/93

SENSORY EVALUATION FOR BREWERS

JEAN-XAVIER GUINARD & IAN ROBERTSON

S ensory evaluation is now recognized as a scientific discipline and has found extensive use in the brewing industry. Its applications include quality assurance, product development, and correlation with chemical, physical, and instrumental measures. In this chapter, we will show how sensory evaluation techniques can be used by brewers. We will also show how homebrewers can benefit from sensory evaluation and turn their homebrew club into a valuable sensory panel.

SENSORY EVALUATION AS A RESEARCH TOOL

Sensory evaluation can be used as a research tool by university researchers, brewing companies, microbrewers, and homebrewers. Its purpose usually is to study the effect of one or several variables on the quality of beer. The development of the proper experimental design, the choice of the appropriate sensory test(s), and the use of the right statistical procedures to analyze the data make a very powerful combination. However, even a small failure at any of these three stages of the research process can have disastrous consequences. It can lead to the mass production of a new product that will not serve its intended purpose, or to a costly and worthless investment to modify the brewing process. One should therefore exercise caution in conducting sensory research and be familiar with sensory evaluation procedures.

Unlike most chemical, physical, and instrumental measurements, sensory evaluation does not require expensive materials and sophisticated equipment. This makes it a valuable tool for the homebrewer. Furthermore, a homebrew club provides a set of motivated and experienced judges, the perfect panel for sensory evaluation experiments.

THE NOTION OF EXPERIMENTAL DESIGN

When a homebrewer wants to study the effect of one variable on beer quality, he or she should keep all variables but the one under study constant. For example, to study the effect of dry-hopping with different hop varieties on beer flavor, one should prepare a single batch of wort, pitch it with yeast, split it into several lots, and then add one variety of hops to each fermentation vessel. The fermentation time and temperature, conditioning, and bottling practices should be the same for all beers. Only then can the homebrewer say that differences in beer flavor are caused by the hop variety used for dry-hopping. The same rule applies for studying any other ingredient's effect on beer quality; i.e., never change more than one ingredient at a time and use the same brewing procedures for all beers.

Illustration by Vicki Hopewell

THE CHOICE OF THE PROPER SENSORY TEST(S)

Research objectives have to be well defined. There are many different types of sensory tests that serve different purposes. The main distinction is between analytical-laboratory tests and consumer tests (Table 1). Analytical tests establish if there are differences among the experimental beers and define the nature and magnitude of these differences. Consumer tests determine acceptance, degree of liking, and preference. These are quite different objectives.

TABLE 1. Types of Sensory Tests

I. ANALYTICAL LABORATORY TESTS

A. Discriminative	B. Quantitative	C. Qualitative

1. Difference tests
  a. Paired comparison
  b. Duo-trio
  c. Triangle
	1. Scaling
	  a. Category
	  b. Ratio
		1. Descriptive analysis
		  a. Flavor profile
		  b. Quantitative descriptive analysis
		  c. Deviation from reference

2. Ranking		
3. Duration a. Time Intensity		

II. AFFECTIVE CONSUMER TESTS

A. Acceptance	B. Preference	C. Hedonic
1. Accept/reject	1. Select one over another option	1. Degree of like/dislike

ANALYTICAL TESTS

Usually, the first step is to determine if the samples, e.g., the beers dry-hopped with different varieties, are different. To answer that question, one can use a variety of discriminative tests, called difference tests. If the nature of the difference among beers is not specified, a duo-trio or a triangle test is used. In the duo-trio test, one sample (the reference) is presented first, followed by two samples one of which is identical to the reference. The judge is asked to find the one identical to the reference. In the triangle test, three samples are simultaneously presented in random order, two of which are identical. The judge is asked to identify the odd sample. When the difference among the beers can be specified, as in "Which beer is more floral?," one should use a pair-test or paired comparison. In this method, two samples are presented simultaneously and the judge is asked to identify the sample with the greater intensity of the specified characteristic. Difference tests should always be conducted using trained, experienced judges. These methods can reliably determine quite small and subtle differences among beers.

Once it has been shown that samples are different, the second step is to define the magnitude of the difference. For this, we use a quantitative procedure such as a scaling method. The intensity of a specified attribute is scored by assigning it a rating on a category or a ratio scale. This allows differences among beers to be reported as numbers. A category scale can be a numerical scale ("score the intensity of bitterness on a scale from 0 to 10, where 0 is none and 10 is extreme bitterness") or a graphic scale (a line anchored with the words "none" and "extreme" or "low" and "high" on which the judge marks the intensity of the rated attribute). When a ratio scale is used, the judge is asked to determine how much higher or lower the intensity of an attribute is compared to a reference. Like difference tests, scaling requires trained judges.

Alternatively, ranking tests can be used when many samples are to be compared. These require judges to arrange a series of samples in an ascending or descending order of intensity for a given attribute. Whereas ranking is simple and can be done by relatively inexperienced judges, it does not determine the magnitude of the differences among samples.

Another technique called time-intensity has found extensive use in sensory research. It quantifies the temporal changes in sensation that occur from the time beer is placed in the mouth until extinction of the sensation. The judge moves a stick along a slot labelled "none" to "extreme." The stick is interfaced to a microcomputer that records intensity vs. time. Using this technique, we have studied the effect of repeated beer ingestion on temporal perception of bitterness (Guinard et al., 1986). It is, however, a method ill-suited for homebrew clubs because it requires expensive hardware and software.

The third step defines the nature of the differences among samples. It is qualitative. Descriptive analysis or "flavor profiling" are the most commonly used techniques. They are based on the fact that a person can be trained to consistently and reproducibly rate the intensities of those attributes that make up the profile under study. A panel of judges trained for flavor profiling is a great asset for a large brewing company as well as for a homebrew club. It can be considered a very reliable instrument and may have a higher sensitivity than most gas chromatographs. For example, the human nose can detect sulfur in beer at concentrations as low as one part per billion (1 microgram per liter).

CONSUMER TESTS

A word about so-called "consumer" tests. They are affective tests. Their purpose is to determine acceptance, preference, and/or degree of liking of a product. They have no analytical value. They are administered using people representative of the target population, i.e., the ultimate users of the product, not trained judges. Such tests include the paired preference test in which two samples are presented to a judge who reports which one he or she prefers. Alternatively, a judge may receive several samples and be asked to rank them according to preference. Another popular method is the hedonic method in which the judge marks his opinion of a product on a nine-point hedonic scale where zero is "dislike extremely" and nine is "like extremely." This method is traditionally used to determine a sample's degree of liking.

The most frequent mistake found in the brewing literature is the use of consumer tests when analytical tests should be used, or vice versa. Assessing the effect of the yeast strain on beer quality by asking consumers (or untrained panelists) which one they prefer is wrong. Difference tests and descriptive analysis by trained judges should be used in that case. Confounding hedonic terms with intensity and/or quality terms also is erroneous. For example, "ideal or objectionable bitterness" (hedonic or subjective terms) is not a substitute for "low or high bitterness" (intensity terms) in qualitative sensory evaluation. Fortunately, the pioneering work of Meilgaard, Pangborn, Clapperton, Mecredy, Neilson, and others has given an edge in sensory evaluation to the brewing industry and the literature is now virtually error-free.

STATISTICS: FRIEND OR FOE?

Statistics combine with sensory evaluation to make a powerful research tool. They allow the researcher to determine the significance of the results by discriminating between actual differences and random error. Generally, for each type of sensory test there is a corresponding statistical test. Tables are available to determine the significance of the results of paired, duo-trio, and triangle tests give the minimum number of correct judgments to establish significance at various probability levels for different tests (Tables 2, 3, and 4).

The probability to give the right answer by chance alone is one-half for a pair-test or a duo-trio and one-third for a triangle test. A one-tailed test is used when there is only one correct answer, e.g., when the judges are asked to determine which sample is more floral. A two-tailed test applies when there is no intuitively correct answer, e.g., when the judges are asked which sample they prefer. If we want to determine whether a beer dry-hopped with Saaz is more floral than one dry-hopped with Chinook, we can have twenty judges in our home-brew club perform a paired comparison.

Checking Table 2, which gives the minimum number of correct judgments to establish significance at the five percent level (traditionally the minimum acceptable level) for a one-tailed test, we find that fifteen out of twenty judges must select the same sample for the difference to be significant. If only fourteen judges select the Chinook sample, we cannot conclude that it is more floral than the Saaz sample. If we want to determine which beer would be liked better by beer drinkers, we can ask a sample of fifty consumers in a bar which beer they prefer.

Table 3 (two-tailed test) indicates that at least thirty-three out of fifty judges must indicate the same preference (Saaz or Chinook) to conclude that one beer is significantly preferred over the other.

To interpret the results of a ranking test, we can consult Table 5, which gives the difference between sums of ranks required for significance at the 5 percent level. For example, if a panel of ten judges ranks five beers for bitterness intensity, two beers will differ significantly in bitterness intensity if the difference between their sum of ranks is higher than twenty.

Misapplication of probability tables for determining significance in paired, duo-trio, and triangle tests are examples of common misuse of statistical procedures in sensory evaluation. The most common mistake is to use a one-tailed test when a two-tailed test should be used or vice versa.

More advanced statistics (analysis of variance, multivariate statistics) are used when a lot of data are collected. They require software that is not readily available to homebrewers. Imagine that the flavor profile (ten attributes) of beers fermented with twenty different yeast strains is determined in duplicate by a trained panel of fifteen judges. This generates six thousand numbers. A type of multivariate analysis called factor analysis is used to boil the information contained in the data down to the main relations among the yeast strains. Factor analysis generates a space in which yeast strains are clustered based on their flavor characteristics in much the same way that a map of the United States would be generated if one fed the distances among American cities to the same computer program. Statistics: friend or foe? Definitely friend, as long as you keep up with them.

SENSORY EVALUATION AS A QUALITY CONTROL AND TROUBLE-SHOOTING TOOL

Flavor profiling and off-flavor detection are two sensory evaluation techniques used to monitor beer quality on a routine basis and to detect sensory defects.

The production of beer with a constant quality is the main concern of large breweries. Similarly, a

TABLE 2. Minimum Numbers of Correct Judgments to Establish Significance at Various Probability Levels for Paired-Comparison and Duo-Trio Tests (one-tailed, p = 1/2)a

PROBABILITY LEVELS

No. of trials (n)	0.05	0.04	0.03	0.02	0.01	0.005	0.001
7	7	7	7	7	7	–	–
8	7	7	8	8	8	8	–
9	8	8	8	8	9	9	–
10	9	9	9	9	10	10	10
11	9	9	10	10	10	11	11
12	10	10	10	10	11	11	12
13	10	11	11	11	12	12	13
14	11	11	11	12	12	13	13
15	12	12	12	12	13	13	14
16	12	12	13	13	14	14	15
17	13	13	13	14	14	15	16
18	13	14	14	14	15	15	16
19	14	14	15	15	15	16	17
20	15	15	15	16	16	17	18
21	15	15	16	16	17	17	18
22	16	16	16	17	17	18	19
23	16	17	17	17	18	19	20
24	17	17	18	18	19	19	20
25	18	18	18	19	19	20	21
26	18	18	19	19	20	20	22
27	19	19	19	20	20	21	22
28	19	20	20	20	21	22	23
29	20	20	21	21	22	22	24
30	20	21	21	22	22	23	24
31	21	21	22	22	23	24	25
32	22	22	22	23	24	24	26
33	22	23	23	23	24	25	26
34	23	23	23	24	25	25	27
35	23	24	24	25	25	26	27
36	24	24	25	25	26	27	28
37	24	25	25	26	26	27	29
38	25	25	26	26	27	28	29
39	26	26	26	27	28	28	30
40	26	27	27	27	28	29	30
41	27	27	27	28	29	30	31
42	27	28	28	29	29	30	32
43	28	28	29	29	30	31	32
44	28	29	29	29	30	31	33
45	29	29	30	30	31	32	34
46	30	30	30	31	32	33	34
47	30	30	31	31	32	33	35
48	31	31	31	32	33	34	36
49	31	32	32	32	33	34	36
50	32	32	33	33	34	35	37
60	37	38	38	39	40	41	43
70	43	43	44	45	46	47	49
80	48	49	49	50	51	52	55
90	54	54	55	56	57	58	61
100	59	60	60	61	63	64	66

a Values (X) not appearing in table may be derived from: $X = (z\sqrt{n} + 1)/2$.

Source: E.B. Roessler et al., Journal of Food Science, 1978, 43, 940–947. Copyright © by Institute of Food Technologists. Reprinted with permission of author and publisher.

TABLE 3. Minimum Numbers of Agreeing Judgments Necessary to Establish Significance at Various Probability Levels for the Paired-Preference Tests (two-tailed, p = 1/2)a

PROBABILITY LEVELS

No. of trials (n)	0.05	0.04	0.03	0.02	0.01	0.005	0.001
7	7	7	7	7	–	–	–
8	8	8	8	8	8	–	–
9	8	8	9	9	9	9	–
10	9	9	9	10	10	10	–
11	10	10	10	10	11	11	11
12	10	10	11	11	11	12	12
13	11	11	11	12	12	12	13
14	12	12	12	12	13	13	14
15	12	12	13	13	13	14	14
16	13	13	13	14	14	14	15
17	13	14	14	14	15	15	16
18	14	14	15	15	15	16	17
19	15	15	15	15	16	16	17
20	15	16	16	16	17	17	18
21	16	16	16	17	17	18	19
22	17	17	17	17	18	18	19
23	17	17	18	18	19	19	20
24	18	18	18	19	19	20	21
25	18	19	19	19	20	20	21
26	19	19	19	20	20	21	22
27	20	20	20	20	21	22	23
28	20	20	21	21	22	22	23
29	21	21	21	22	22	23	24
30	21	22	22	22	23	24	25
31	22	22	22	23	24	24	25
32	23	23	23	23	24	25	26
33	23	23	24	24	25	25	27
34	24	24	24	25	25	26	27
35	24	25	25	25	26	27	28
36	25	25	25	26	27	27	29
37	25	26	26	26	27	28	29
38	26	26	27	27	28	29	30
39	27	27	27	28	28	29	31
40	27	27	28	28	29	30	31
41	28	28	28	29	30	30	32
42	28	29	29	29	30	31	32
43	29	29	30	30	31	32	33
44	29	30	30	30	31	32	34
45	30	30	31	31	32	33	34
46	31	31	31	32	33	33	35
47	31	31	32	32	33	34	36
48	32	32	32	33	34	35	36
49	32	33	33	34	34	35	37
50	33	33	34	34	35	36	37
60	39	39	39	40	41	42	44
70	44	45	45	46	47	48	50
80	50	50	51	51	52	53	56
90	55	56	56	57	58	59	61
100	61	61	62	63	64	65	67

TABLE 4. Minimum Numbers of Correct Judgments to Establish Significance at Various Probability Levels for the Triangle Tests (one-tailed, p = 1/3)b

PROBABILITY LEVELS

No. of trials (n)	0.05	0.04	0.03	0.02	0.01	0.005	0.001
5	4	5	5	5	5	5	–
6	5	5	5	5	6	6	–
7	5	6	6	6	6	7	7
8	6	6	6	6	7	7	8
9	6	7	7	7	7	8	8
10	7	7	7	7	8	8	9
11	7	7	8	8	8	9	10
12	8	8	8	8	9	9	10
13	8	8	9	9	9	10	11
14	9	9	9	9	10	10	11
15	9	9	10	10	10	11	12
16	9	10	10	10	11	11	12
17	10	10	10	11	11	12	13
18	10	11	11	11	12	12	13
19	11	11	11	12	12	13	14
20	11	11	12	12	13	13	14
21	12	12	12	13	13	14	15
22	12	12	13	13	14	14	15
23	12	13	13	13	14	15	16
24	13	13	13	14	15	15	16
25	13	14	14	14	15	16	17
26	14	14	14	15	15	16	17
27	14	14	15	15	16	17	18
28	15	15	15	16	16	17	18
29	15	15	16	16	17	17	19
30	15	16	16	16	17	18	19
31	16	16	16	17	18	18	20
32	16	16	17	17	18	19	20
33	17	17	17	18	18	19	21
34	17	17	18	18	19	20	21
35	17	18	18	19	19	20	22
36	18	18	18	19	20	20	22
37	18	18	19	19	20	21	22
38	19	19	19	20	21	21	23
39	19	19	20	20	21	22	23
40	19	20	20	21	21	22	24
41	20	20	20	21	22	23	24
42	20	20	21	21	22	23	25
43	20	21	21	22	23	24	25
44	21	21	22	22	23	24	26
45	21	22	22	23	24	24	26
46	22	22	22	23	24	25	27
47	22	22	23	23	24	25	27
48	22	23	23	24	25	26	27
49	23	23	24	24	25	26	28
50	23	24	24	25	26	26	28
60	27	27	28	29	30	31	33
70	31	31	32	33	34	35	37
80	35	35	36	36	38	39	41
90	38	39	40	40	42	43	45
100	42	43	43	44	45	47	49

b Values (X) not appearing in table may be derived from: $X = 0.4714 \, z\sqrt{n} + [(2n + 3)/6]$.

TABLE 5. Difference Between Sums of Ranks*
Required for Significance at the 5% Level (Hollander and Wolfe, 1973)

Number of judges	Number of samples							
	3	4	5	6	7	8	9	10
3	6	8	10	13	15	18	20	22
4	7	10	12	15	18	21	24	26
5	8	11	14	17	20	23	27	30
6	9	12	15	19	22	26	29	33
7	9	13	16	20	24	28	32	36
8	10	14	18	22	26	30	34	38
9	10	15	19	23	27	32	36	41
10	11	15	20	24	29	34	38	43
11	11	16	21	26	30	35	40	45
12	12	17	21	27	32	37	42	48
13	12	18	23	28	33	39	44	50
14	13	18	24	29	34	40	46	52
15	13	19	24	30	36	42	47	53

*Add up the ranks obtained by each beer. Then compare the difference between the sum of ranks of two beers to the value shown in the table. If the difference is higher, the two beers are significantly different.

homebrewer may want to be able to make the same product repeatedly. In both cases, the brewer must resort to using flavor profiling to define and then keep track of his product's flavor. Flavor profiling is a very powerful technique when properly used; a waste of time and energy otherwise. Extreme care must be exercised in (1) selecting the descriptors of the flavor attributes; and (2) training the panel. The descriptors used must have a universal meaning and carry no affective or hedonic value. Ideally, they should be translatable in any language. This means that no subjective descriptors such as balanced/unbalanced, good/bad, young/mature should be used. Such terms have different meaning for different people. Also, standards should be available that correspond to each descriptor. For example, a few microliters of diacetyl can be added to beer to make a standard for "buttery." Similarly, a bitterness standard can be prepared by spiking a beer with iso-alpha-acids (isomerized hop extract).

The panel, e.g., brewery employees or homebrew club members, must be trained to evaluate the attributes with consistency and reproducibility. Consistency is the measure of agreement among the judges; reproducibility is their ability to give the same ratings to the same beer on different occasions. Provided that one dedicated member is willing to prepare standards, a homebrew club can train to be a skilled panel in a few sessions. A standard scorecard can then be designed and adopted which will include between eight and fifteen sensory attributes. The attributes might be limited to flavor properties only or might also encompass appearance, aroma, flavor (aroma and taste), and tactile properties. Such a scorecard can be used for all the beers made by the brewery or homebrew club, or a specific scorecard can be designed for the different types of beers to be evaluated on a regular basis, i.e., one for ales, one for lagers, one for Lambics, etc. For a very well-documented glossary of beer flavor descriptors see page 12. The scorecard that we use at University of California at Davis for some applications is reproduced in Figure 1.

Off-flavor detection is similar to flavor profiling except that it focuses on defective flavors. A panel trained to detect and recognize off-flavors using various standards is a valuable tool for troubleshooting. For example, standards can be prepared by spoiling wort or beer with pure cultures of various contaminants, e.g., Pediococcus, Brettanomyces, etc., or by spiking beer with various undesirable chemicals, e.g., H_2S, dimethyl sulfide, diacetyl, guaiacol, etc. If the panel can consistently recognize these characters, the source of the off-flavor often can be identified and corrected faster than with more laborious instrumental methods of analysis.

The following conclusions should be drawn from this review of sensory procedures. Sensory

U.C. Davis Scorecard for Descriptive Analysis

NAME_____

Please rate the intensity of the following parameters using a scale from 0 to 10 (0=none; 10=extreme).

ATTRIBUTE Sample Code				
AROMA				
Fruity				
Floral				
Oxidized				
Grassy				
Grainy				
Phenolic/medicinal				
Diacetyl/buttery				
Yeasty				
Sulfury				
Skunky/light struck				
TASTE				
Bitter				
Sour				
Sweet				
Metallic				
TEXTURE				
Carbonation				
Astringency				

FIGURE 1. U.C. Davis Scorecard for Descriptive Analysis

TABLE 6. Sensory Evaluation for the Homebrew Club

Panel:	Homebrew club members. The number of judges depends on the nature of the test. At least fifteen are needed for difference tests and five for flavor profiling. Use judges of demonstrated ability.
Locale:	Well-lighted room, free of extraneous odors, noise, and bright colors. Temperature around 70 degrees F (21 degrees C).
Equipment:	Ideally, judges should be separated in order not to influence each other. Partitions can be placed on a large table to make booths. Use clean beer glasses. A recurved shape retains volatiles better. Samples are coded with three-digit numbers to minimize biases.
Time of day:	Avoid tasting right after meals. Less important than panel motivation.
Serving temperature:	Anywhere between 50 and 65 degrees F (10 and 18.5 degrees C), depending on the type of beer to be evaluated. Avoid large (5 degrees F) variations in temperature among samples.
Number of samples:	For difference tests, keep number of pairs, duo-trios, or triangles below ten; fatigue might set in otherwise. Ranking gets difficult above six samples. For flavor profiling, five samples is a maximum, especially if the number of attributes to rate is high (ten or more).
Training:	Perform difference, ranking, and scaling tests on commercial samples. For flavor profiling, prepare standards for each attribute. The panel should check them until it is very familiar with all of them. Do flavor profiles of commercial beers on several occasions. Check judges for consistency (agreement with rest of panel) and reproducibility. Train judges to recognize common off-flavors by preparing adequate samples.

evaluation techniques can provide valuable information if they are used in the right way. The distinction between analytical and consumer tests should be kept in mind. Not only large brewing companies but also microbreweries and homebrew clubs can successfully develop sensory evaluation programs. The applications for research, quality control, new product development, and troubleshooting are many.

A condensation of guidelines for the use of sensory procedures by a homebrew club is presented in Table 6.

PREPARING OF REFERENCE STANDARDS FOR FLAVOR PROFILING

Joint working groups of the American Society of Brewing Chemists, the European Brewery Convention, and the Master Brewers Association of the Americas have developed a beer flavor terminology (Meilgaard et al., 1979) for use in flavor profiling. Based on this work, Noonan and Papazian (1988) have proposed guidelines for beer aroma recognition (see page 14). Indeed, one of the basic principles of the system of flavor terminology is that the meaning of each term is illustrated with reference standards. Ideally, pure chemicals are used in the preparation of standards to ensure that each term is used in the exact way by all users of the flavor wheel. It is reasonable to assume that pure chemicals do not vary too much in flavor around the world.

However, the preparation of standards with pure chemicals has several drawbacks for homebrewers: (1) pure chemicals can be expensive; (2) they are not always readily available; and (3) they may be difficult to handle (a fume hood and micropipettes are usually required). Furthermore, the standards suggested by Meilgaard et al. (1982) are prepared using a single pure chemical in a base beer. A significant problem with this approach is the inability of a single compound to faithfully reproduce a complex aroma characteristic, such as grassy or floral.

Consequently, based on our routine use of flavor profiling for research or teaching, we suggest the use of foodstuffs or raw materials readily available throughout the world during most seasons for the preparation of reference standards. Note that the list of terms differs slightly from the original list given by Meilgaard (1979).

A twelve-ounce bottle of neutral beer (commercial light beer in long-neck bottles) is used for the preparation of most standards. Open the bottle, spike with the appropriate material, recap, and incubate for at least a few hours before use (ideally overnight) at cool temperature (50 degrees F or 10 degrees C). Once the standards have been poured, it is best to cover the glasses with Petri dishes to better retain the volatiles.

As mentioned by Noble et al. (1987), the intensity of a reference standards will vary with its function. To define a specific term, an intensity that provides a very obvious aroma is recommended. On the other hand, to train judges for flavor profiling, lower intensities are needed to better illustrate that aroma characteristic at the level at which it may be found in beer. Also, it is often appropriate to combine terms to describe a particular flavor characteristic (for example, rose/violet as a floral term, or peach/apricot as a fruity term). In such a case, a dual standard is prepared.

TABLE 7. Flavor Descriptors and Reference Standards

General descriptor	Specific descriptor	Reference standard (in 12 oz. beer unless otherwise specified)
Alcoholic	Alcohol	15 ml of 95% ethanol
Spicy	Clove	2 cloves
Floral	Geranium	Piece of geranium leaf
	Violet	Few crushed violet petals
	Rose	Few crushed rose petals
Hoppy	Hops	Few pellets of fresh hops (1 standard per variety)
Fruity	Lemon	10 ml juice and peel
	Grapefruit	10 ml juice and peel
	Orange	10 ml juice and peel
	Raspberry	4-5 crushed raspberries
	Black currant	15 ml Ribena® or cassis cream
	Cherry	15 ml brine of canned cherries
	Peach	30 ml peach nectar
	Pear	30 ml pear nectar
	Melon	1-3 tbsp mashed fresh canteloupe
	Apple	30 ml apple juice
	Banana	2 slices of banana
	Artificial fruit	1 tsp tropical punch Kool-Aid®
Winy	Wine	50 ml of jug white wine
Vegetative	Grassy	Freshly-cut grass (no beer)
	Hay/Straw	Finely-cut pieces of hay-straw (no beer)
	Tea	5-10 flakes of black tea
	Tobacco	5-10 flakes of tobacco
Cooked vegetable	Green beans	15 ml brine from canned green beans
	Asparagus	10 ml brine from canned asparagus
Grainy	Malt	Handful of kernels or 2 tbsp of
	Barley	mashed grain in a glass (no beer)
	Wheat	
	Rice	
	Corn	
Worty	Wort	1:1 wort/beer
Caramel	Honey	3 tbsp of honey
	Butterscotch	2 cut Kraft® caramels
	Buttery	Few drops of imitation butter-flavored extract
	Licorice	Few pieces of licorice twists
	Soy	3 ml soy sauce
	Chocolate	Few drops of chocolate-flavored extract or 2 tsp powdered cocoa

	Molasses	1 tsp molasses
	Coffee	1/2 tsp ground coffee
Nutty	Walnut	10 crushed walnuts
	Almond	Few drops of almond extract
Pungent	Ethyl acetate	Few drops of nail polish remover
	Acetic acid	15 ml white vinegar
Sulfury	H_2S	Yolk of hard-boiled egg (no beer)
	Cabbage	10 ml brine from boiled cabbage leaves
	Sweet corn	15 ml brine from canned corn
	Burnt match	Tips of 3 burnt wooden matches
	Rubber	2 small pieces of rubber tubing
	Lightstruck	Leave clear bottle in sun
Yeasty	Yeast	Few mls of fresh yeast slurry
Oxidized hours	Oxidized	Incubate beer at 100° F (38° C) for a few
Soapy	Soap	Few flakes of Ivory® soap
Earthy	Mushroom	2 chopped mushrooms
	Moldy	Slice of moldy bread (no beer)
Papery	Cardboard	Few pieces of cardboard
Petroleum	Plastic	Few pieces of cut up plastic tubing
	Tar	Few drops of roofing tar
	Gasoline	2-3 drops of gasoline
Burnt	Smoky	2-3 drops of smoky flavor extract
	Burnt toast	Few pieces of burnt toast
Medicinal	Phenolic	0.1 ml guaiacol
Lactic	Lactic	10 ml brine from canned sauerkraut
Cheesy	Cheese	Few crumbles of feta cheese
Meaty	Meaty	10 ml beef broth
Fishy	Shrimp	3 ml shrimp brine
Sweet	Sugar	5 g sucrose
Sour	Acid	5 g citric acid
Salty	Salt	1 g sodium chloride
Bitter	Iso-alpha-acids	Few drops of isomerized hop extract
Astringent	Tannins	3 g alum or grape seed tannin
Viscous	Viscous	1 tablespoon of Polycose®
Body	Body	15 g of dextrins

REFERENCES

Guinard, J.-X.; R.M. Pangborn; and M.J. Lewis (1986). "Effect of repeated ingestion on temporal perception of bitterness in beer." J. Am. Soc. Brew. Chem. 44:28-32.

Hollander, M., and D.A. Wolfe, "Nonparametric Statistical Methods," Wiley, New York; 1973.

Meilgaard, M.C.; C.E. Dalgliesh; and J.F. Clapperton (1979). "Beer flavor terminology." J. Am. Soc. Brew. Chem. 37:47-52.

Meilgaard, M.C.; D.S. Reid; and K.A. Wuborski (1982). "Reference standards for beer flavor terminology system." J. Am. Soc. Brew. Chem. 40:119-128.

Noble, A.C.; R.A. Arnold; J. Buechsenstein; E.J. Leach; J.O. Schmidt, and P.M. Stern (1987). "Modification of a standardized system of wine aroma terminology." Am. J. Enol. Vitic. 38:143-146.

Noonan, G., and C. Papazian (1988). Aroma ID kit development. Tenth Annual Conference on Quality Beer and Brewing. Denver, Colo.

BEER FLAVOR IN YOUR BREWERY

RON SIEBEL

Updated 1993 by Ilse Shelton,
Siebel Institute of Technology

The topic of this chapter is beer flavor, and specifically, how it is measured. I'd like to first address the need for tasting, and then some preliminaries for setting up a beer-flavor profile. This information is a very good tool in controlling beer flavor.

I'll spend the bulk of my time looking at a method of flavor profiling that was introduced to the industry in the 1960s. It was the first working profile in use in this country, and is still being used by a number of breweries. We at the Siebel Institute have updated it, however, and always consider changes to improve it further.

Finally, I'll comment briefly on the most important factor in flavor tasting: the individual taster.

There are three important factors from the standpoint of tasting, the first of which is evaluation. Evaluating beer means going beyond simply asking if it is good or bad, do you like it or not. Evaluating is asking which components of your beer make it different from others, and how you can regulate the intensity of natural components — for example, the amount of hoppiness, bitterness, maltiness, etc. — to achieve the flavor you want.

Consistency is another factor that has caused brewers difficulty over the years. Consistency can be very elusive, but is probably the most important factor from a consumer's standpoint. Therefore, it is necessary that you taste and profile your beer in order to detect minor changes in flavor and to monitor the consistency.

Finally, defects are important to identify so they can be isolated and corrected. For example, if you start detecting taste thresholds of diacetyl in your beer, you may wish to check your fermentation cycle and correct it before the taste becomes so manifest that it is detectable by consumers.

Glossary of Beer-Flavor Attributes

Fruity	Perfumy fruit flavor resembling apples.
Hoppy	Flavor due to aromatic hop constituents.
Bitter	Bitter taste derived from hops.
Malty	Aromatic flavor due to malt.
Hang	Lingering bitterness or harshness.
Tart	Taste sensation caused by acids, e.g. vinegar or lemon.
Oxidized	Stale beer flavor. Resembles paperlike or cardboardlike flavor.
Medicinal	Chemical or phenolic flavor, at times resembling solvent.
Sulfur	Skunky — odor of beer exposed to sunlight.
	Sulfur Dioxide — taste/odor of burnt matches.
	Hydrogen Sulfide — odor of rotten eggs.
	Onion — reminiscent of fresh or cooked onions.
Bacterial	A general term covering off-flavors such as moldy, musty, woody, lactic acid, vinegar, or microbiological spoilage.
Yeasty	Reminiscent of yeast, bouillon, or glutamic acid.
Diacetyl	Typical butterlike flavor. The odor of cottage cheese.
Mouthfeel	Sensation derived from the consistency or viscosity of a beer. For example, thin or heavy.

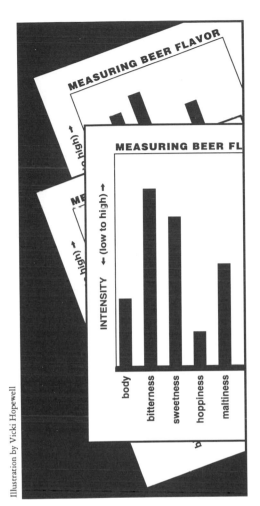

The glossary of beer-flavor attributes gives us definitions for specific flavors but is by no means inclusive. You need to build your own list of the attributes that are applicable to your situation, and the definitions that are meaningful to your tasters. If you set up a flavor profile, keep the number of attributes to a reasonable number. You're better off dealing with fewer attributes and doing the job well than trying to taste a whole range.

These are some suggestions for definitions you might use when you first begin to develop a flavor profile.

The profiling system the Siebel Institute uses is not meant to be a standard, but it has been used successfully for many years. One of the first things that must be done is setting up an overall rating system. We use a nine-point hedonic scale, which runs from plus four to minus four, with zero being neutral.

9-POINT SCALE OF PREFERENCE

+4 Like extremely

ı3 Like very much

+2 Like moderately

+1 Like slightly

0 Neither like nor dislike

-1   Dislike slightly

-2   Dislike moderately

-3   Dislike very much

-4   Dislike extremely

I recommend being as descriptive as you can in your overall ratings to help your panels be as descriptive as possible.

EXAMPLE OF A GRADING SYSTEM TO BE USED IN PROFILE EVALUATION OF A BEER

+4   The highest mark the taster can give. A sound, clean beer that strikes the taster "just at the right moment." A grade this high reflects strong personal preference.

+3   A sound, clean beer and one for which the taster shows some personal preference. These preferences, such as the correct hop character, excellent aromatic quality, etc., should be clearly stated, if possible.

+2   An average, sound, clean, salable beer. If the taster can find nothing wrong with the beer, it should receive a "+2" rating and one should suppress his personal likes and dislikes for a thin or heavy beer, bitter or sweet, etc.

+1   A sound, clean beer and one which has no abnormal faults, but the taster feels some normal tastes are a little more pronounced (too bitter, too sweet, etc.) or a little too subdued (less hop, less body, etc.) than generally found. A faint trace of "normal" fault such as slight oxidation or a little too much of an SO_2 character is permitted.

0   A beer in which you can find nothing in particular to praise and nothing in particular to fault. It can have faults but not of an intensity to cause the taster to reject the beer. A neutral type of beer.

-1   A beer with some abnormal defects present but at a mild level. The taster does not like the beer, but does not seriously reject it. A beer that is stale or abnormally harsh or slightly lightstruck or has a thermal induced character belongs here.

-2   Abnormal defects present, such as diacetyl, thermal-induced taste, lightstruck, can liner, medicinal, etc., at an easily detectable level, and the salability of the beer is questioned.

-3   Abnormal flavors present at a high intensity and probably cannot be eliminated by blending or the use of activated carbon. An objectionable beer.

-4   Undrinkable beer. You'll know it when you taste it.

Page 80 shows our actual Taste Test Form. In tasting, we measure a total of thirty-five attributes, which might be a little too much for anyone not trained. The first five at the top are all compulsory qualities. When the taster profiles the beer, he must evaluate those qualities and make a mark in the category, based on the plus or minus for the type and style of beer. For example, if he's tasting a lager beer, he'd judge it as an American lager. As such, it would be either staler or fresher than a normal lager beer; it would be thinner or fuller in body than a normal lager beer, etc.

Siebel Institute of Technology Taste Test Form

Taste Panel ID _____ Date _____   1st 2nd 3rd 4th E W

Taster Name _____   A B C D E F G H I J K L M N O P Q R S T U V W X Y Z

	1	2	3	4	5	6	7
Identity (Brand)							
Lab. No.							
Stale, OXID. ◄──► Fresh							
Thin ◄── BODY ──► Full							
Less ◄ FLAVORFUL ► More							
HARSH ◄──► SMOOTH							
Low ← HOP INTENSITY → Hi							
Vinous							
Fruity, estery							
Spicy							
Aley							
Alcoholic							
BITTER, total							
Afterbitter							
SWEET							
Malty							
Caramel							
DRY							
Astringent							
Husk, Grainy							
Worty							
Sulfitic (SO_2)							
Sulfidic (H_2S, R-SH)							
YEASTY							
DMS, cooked vegetable							
Light struck, skunky							
Musty, cellar, woody							
Syrupy							
Cardboard, papery							
Burnt, scorched, bready							
Aldehydic							
Infected							
Diacetyl							
Sour							
Metallic							
Medicinal, phenolic							
Foreign (Describe)							
AROMA							
OTHER PROPERTIES							
RATINGS	1 2 3 4 ⊟ 0 ½	1 2 3 4 ⊟ 0 ½	1 2 3 4 ⊟ 0 ½	1 2 3 4 ⊟ 0 ½	1 2 3 4 ⊟ 0 ½	1 2 3 4 ⊟ 0 ½	1 2 3 4 ⊟ 0 ½

The other compulsory marks are bitter and afterbitter, found in the middle of the sheet. Again, those are rated on the average for each particular type of beer.

The taster mentally changes this scale when he profiles a malt liquor, an ale, or a European lager. Obviously you can't compare an American lager to another style of beer or a European lager. So the taster must shift gears.

Except for the seven attributes listed, every attribute is a voluntary marking. If the taster gets an impression, he notes the intensity level from one (mild) to four (strong).

Every attribute that falls below "yeasty" on this chart is considered a negative attribute or a defect.

There is also a place to comment on hop quality, odor, and other properties. These are the taster's personal comments, made in addition to marking off the attributes and intensities.

The sheet should have a place for taster identi-fication. We use a code, and date the sheet. We run three or four panels in a day, so we also indicate the panel and which side we tasted on.

This is an interesting point: we have ten tasters on our panel. We serve two packages of beer, so five people taste from each package. The obvious reason is that we can't get enough beer out of one package. The unobvious reason is that there is occasionally package-to-package variation. It can be caused by high air in the package, for example. If we run into this situation, we have a retaste to determine how serious the variation is.

We rate up to seven beers on a panel. Beyond that number, the acuity of the taster diminishes. On the taste sheet, each column represents a different beer. Please consult the sheet on page 82. If there are no markings at the top, as in columns one, two,

Siebel Institute of Technology Taste Test Form

Taste Panel ID **H** Date **8/24**

Taster Name _____

1st 2nd 3rd 4th E W

A B C D E F G H I J K L M N O P Q R S T U V W X Y Z

	1	2	3	4	5	6	7
Identity (Brand)			ALE	ML	LITE		
Lab. No.							
Stale, OXID. ◄—► Fresh							
Thin ◄—BODY—► Full							
Less◄FLAVORFUL►More							
HARSH ◄—►SMOOTH							
Low◄HOP INTENSITY►Hi							
Vinous							
Fruity, estery							
Spicy							
Aley							
Alcoholic							
BITTER, total							
Afterbitter							
SWEET							
Malty							
Caramel							
DRY							
Astringent							
Husk, Grainy							
Worty							
Sulfitic (SO_2)							
Sulfidic (H_2S, R-SH)							
YEASTY							
DMS, cooked vegetable							
Light struck, skunky							
Musty, cellar, woody							
Syrupy							
Cardboard, papery							
Burnt, scorched, bready							
Aldehydic							
Infected							
Diacetyl							
Sour							
Metallic							
Medicinal, phenolic							
Foreign (Describe)							
AROMA					stale		
OTHER PROPERTIES							
RATINGS	1 2 3 4 / 0	1 2 3 4 / 0	1 2 3 4 / 0	1 2 3 4 / 0	1 2 3 4 / 0	1 2 3 4 / 0	1 2 3 4 / 0

six, and seven, the beer is an American lager. As you can see, the beer in the third column is an ale, in the fourth a malt liquor, in the fifth a light beer. The brackets around columns one and two mean that tasters should specifically compare these two.

Normally, we drink the lighter beers first, moving on through the heavier beers — although on this taste sheet, it has been requested not to be that way.

All the compulsory categories have been marked. The shaded rectangle position represents the average for that type and style of beer. The first spaces note the minus and the last spaces represent the plus from the average.

At the bottom of the flavor profile is a numerical rating which is the nine-point hedonic scale mentioned earlier.

The Siebel Taste Test Form on page 82 is the actual form used after the taste panel evaluation. Seven beers were evaluated. Number one, two, six, and seven are the American lagers, number three an ale, number four a malt liquor, and number five a light beer.

In looking at the attributes of each beer, sample number one is an average American lager with no off-flavors and rates a plus 2.5. However number two shows oxidation with 2 intensity units of papery, bready, and aldehydic. There are also infected notes, diacetyl and sour and the beer was rated a minus 3. Clearly, the first lager is far superior. Sample number three, the ale, has more body and higher hop intensity. It shows a higher bitterness intensity than the average ale. The ale is also slightly oxidized and thus rates 1 intensity unit bready. The overall rating is a plus 1. The malt liquor, number four, shows all the normal malt liquor characteristics: sweet, alcoholic, higher esters, no detectable off-flavors, and a rating of plus

2.5. Number five, the light beer, is very stale and oxidized with 2 intensity units skunky but no infection. The beer has received a minus rating but not as low as the infected beer number two.

Once the evaluation sheet is turned in, the data is scanned by computer and a printout is received (see the Taste Panel Profile on page 86). Along the top of the sheet is the individual code for each of the eight tasters. If they made no response, a zero is entered, if they did respond, the level of intensity is marked with one, two, three, or four. At the bottom of each column is the number rating the taster gave the beer, as well as an overall rating for the beer. So, simply and quickly one can see the total intensity levels, the overall rating, the panel distribution, and any comments made by the taster. From this sheet the panel leader, who is responsible for the final report, will develop a final summary comment. The panel leader understands each individual taster's acuity. If someone is very sensitive to diacetyl, for example, it will be noted and given more weight. The final computerized printout of the Initial Taste Profile is on page 87. The profile visually expresses the profile summary. All relatively normal attributes show their intensity units with solid dots. Below the term 'yeasty' is the listing of taste defects. Defect intensity units are denoted with stars. The numbers following the symbols note the intensity units (IU) and the number of tasters that commented.

The profile gives a clear overall analysis of the beer and is a particularly good format for comparing different beers.

In establishing the panel, make it a point to recruit people who have time to serve. Tasters need to be available and need to take the job seriously. Next, orient them to what you expect of them, giving them procedures, terminologies, profiles you use, etc.

Training is very important in establishing the panel. You must familiarize your panelists with the various tastes in beer, and explain the flavor evaluation vocabulary so everyone is speaking in the same terms. For example, they have to interpret "musty" as you do. Doctor a beer, let the panelists taste it, and then discuss it. Later you can test to determine levels of acuity.

As odd as it might sound, tasting a beer on a routine basis two and three times daily can become mundane. You have to keep your panelists motivated.

Performance is the key to good, successful tastings. You must monitor your panelists, and occasionally retest them to see that their acuities in different tastes have not diminished.

In selecting your panelists, choose people who are interested. If someone doesn't want to taste, don't force him or her into it. Health is pertinent. If the individual has allergies or health problems, that person will not be able to taste as well as someone who is healthy.

As in beer, the best taster is consistent. The taster must be so accurate and consistent that the person can duplicate results. You will find this out by doing periodic testing.

The panel should be held in a clean, quiet, well-lighted location. A cluttered office or a coffee room is not suitable. It should be pleasant, as the surroundings will definitely affect your tasters. It should also be convenient.

You certainly want a taste environment that is free from odors, as odors can have a residual effect. If there are lingering odors from cleaning solvents, tasters will not give accurate results.

SIEBEL INST. OF TECHNOLOGY

Taste panel profile on Duesseldorfer Amber Ale
Lab number: 501904
Initial Tasting, Tested August 27, 1993
Received August 25, 1993

	d	y	j	q	b	s	h	z	Total
Stale←OXIDATION→Fresh	-1	-1	-3	-1	0	-1	-	-2	-11
Thin ←BODY→Full	0	0	1	1	1	-1	1	-1	3
Less←FLAVORFUL→More	0	1	-2	1	0	0	0	0	0
Harsh←PALATE→Smooth	-1	0	-2	-1	0	0	0	-1	-6
Low←HOP INTENSITY→Hi	1	0	2	1	1	0	0	-1	5
Vinous	3	0	0	2	0	0	0	0	6
Fruity, estery	2	0	0	2	1	1	3	1	13
Spicy	0	0	0	0	1	0	0	0	1
Aley	0	0	0	0	1	0	0	0	1
Alcoholic	0	0	0	1	0	0	0	0	1
BITTER, total	3	2	4	3	3	3	3	2	29
Afterbitter	3	2	4	3	2	3	3	2	28
SWEET	0	1	0	0	1	0	0	0	3
Malty	1	0	0	1	0	0	0	0	3
Caramel	1	1	0	0	2	0	0	0	5
DRY	3	0	0	2	0	0	2	0	9
Astringent	3	1	0	2	0	0	0	1	9
Husk, grainy	0	2	0	0	1	0	0	0	4
Worty	0	0	0	0	0	0	0	0	0
Sulfitic (SO$_2$)	2	0	0	0	0	0	0	0	3
Sulfidic (H$_2$S, R-SH)	2	0	0	0	0	0	0	0	3
YEASTY	1	0	0	0	0	0	0	0	1
DMS, cooked vegetable	0	0	0	1	1	0	1	0	4
Light-struck, skunky	0	0	0	0	0	0	0	0	0
Musty, cellar, woody	0	2	1	0	0	0	0	0	4
Syrupy	0	0	0	0	0	0	0	0	0
Cardboard, papery	1	0	0	0	0	0	0	2	4
Burnt, scorched, bready	1	1	3	1	1	1	0	0	10
Aldehydic	0	0	3	0	0	0	0	0	4
Infected	0	0	1	0	0	0	1	0	3
Diacetyl	1	1	0	0	0	0	2	2	8
Sour	1	0	0	0	0	0	0	0	1
Metallic	0	0	0	0	0	0	0	0	0
Medicinal, phenolic	0	0	0	0	0	0	0	1	1
Foreign, off	0	0	0	0	0	0	0	0	0
Panel rating	-1.0	-1.0	-2.0	+1.5	+0.5	+0.5	+0.5	-0.5	-0.2
Distribution	5 / 0 / 5								

Panelist	Hop qualities	Aroma	Other properties
d			
y			
j			
q			
b			
s			

j q b — *Stale, oxidized flavor. Harsh and astringent. Malty with DMS notes.*

SIEBEL INSTITUTE OF TECHNOLOGY
4055 West Peterson Ave., Chicago, IL 60646 (312) 463-3400

INITIAL TASTE PROFILE

Lab number : 501904
Identity : Duesseldorfer Amber Ale
Customer code :
Date received : July 24, 1986
Date tested : July 25, 1986

	Average
Stale‹ OXIDATION→Fresh	✶✶✶✶✶✶✶✶✶✶✶ -11 IU
Thin ◄——BODY——➤ Full	●●● 3 IU
Less←FLAVORFUL→More	0 IU
Harsh←PALATE→Smooth	●●●●●● -6 IU
Low←HOP INTENSITY ›Hi	●●●●● 5 IU
Vinous	●●●●●● 6 IU, 3 Panelists
Fruity, estery	●●●●●●●●●●●●● 13 IU, 8
Spicy	● 1 IU, 1
Aley	● 1 IU, 1
Alcoholic	● 1 IU, 1
BITTER, total	●●●●●●●●●●●●●●●●●●●●●●●●●●●●● 29 IU, 10
Afterbitter	●●●●●●●●●●●●●●●●●●●●●●●●●●●● 28 IU, 10
SWEET	●●● 3 IU, 3
Malty	●●● 3 IU, 3
Caramel	●●●●● 5 IU, 4
DRY	●●●●●●●●● 9 IU, 4
Astringent	●●●●●●●●● 9 IU, 5
Husk, grainy	●●●● 4 IU, 3
Worty	
Sulfitic (SO$_2$)	●●● 3 IU, 1
Sulfidic (H$_2$S, R-SH)	●●● 3 IU, 1
YEASTY	● 1 IU, 1
DMS, cooked vegetable	✶✶✶✶ 4 IU, 4
Light-struck, skunky	
Musty, cellar, moody	✶✶✶✶ 4 IU, 3
Syrupy	
Cardboard, papery	✶✶✶✶ 4 IU, 3
Burnt, scorched, bready	✶✶✶✶✶✶✶✶✶✶ 10 IU, 8
Aldonydlo	✶✶✶✶ 4 IU, 1
Infected	✶✶✶✶ 3 IU, 3
Diacetyl	✶✶✶✶✶✶✶✶ 8 IU, 5
Sour	✶ 1 IU, 1
Metallic	
Medicinal, phenolic	✶ 1 IU, 1
Foreign, off	

Panel rating: - 0.2

Panel distribution: 5 / 0 / 5

Comments: Stale, oxidized flavor. Harsh and astringent. Malty with DMS notes.

Reviewed by: Ilse Shelton

(C) Siebel Institute of Technology
Approval Needed for Reproduction

One factor for consideration in setting up the panel is the color of the beer glasses. We at Siebel Institute use ruby red glasses, for example, because we don't want panelists to evaluate the physical characteristics of the beer — i.e., the foam, clarity, color, etc. — during tasting. They are there to taste and taste only. Physical qualities are quantified in the lab.

Our panelists normally drink beer starting with the one on the left and move toward the right. Therefore we place the lighter beers on the left, so tasters move from lighter to heavier progressively.

You should also give your panelists special instructions if there are any. We list them on a blackboard, rather than state them. There are also a few panel rules. We ask the tasters to refrain from making comments during the actual taste test. This includes smacking lips or retching. We also ask panelists to be on time to tastings, so that the test is not disrupted or postponed.

Finally, no taster is allowed to change his marks once the test is over. When each panelist is finished, he lays the sheet down. When everyone has finished, they discuss the beer.

No matter how large or small your brewery is, you don't need expensive or complicated tasting equipment to conduct a valid testing. In fact, you already have the most sophisticated instrumentation for tasting beer — your own sense of taste and smell. The only problem in a smaller brewery is that you have fewer people to rely on for tastings. Perhaps you can exchange beers with someone for tasting, or periodically send your beers out.

Brewers should train themselves to evaluate beer. If there is one thing I'd do in running a brewery, it is get very proficient in identifying certain flavors, and particularly defect flavors. Then I could recognize them when they first occurred, hopefully in time to take action.

Finally, producing a high-quality beer, consistently, is the best thing you can do to ensure the sale of your beer.

ORIGINS OF NORMAL
AND ABNORMAL FLAVOR

TED KONIS

I 'd like this to be a very important lesson for you and a guide throughout your brewing career. This chapter is about the origins of normal and abnormal flavors in beer, and to complement this, I'll refer to the Siebel computerized flavor profile. The profile is made out for ABC Brewing Company, the brewmaster of which is Mr. Henry Suds who received a minus 1.6 rating.

In our Siebel rating scale, we go on a hedonic scale of minus 4 being undrinkable to plus 4 being excellent. This is a technical — not a consumer — taste panel. We are trained to look for defects. The very good American beers have a rating of plus 2 to 2.5. With the homebrewers and microbrewers coming into the industry, the ratings have escalated to plus 3 to 3.5. They are unusual, positive, excellent beers. The Siebel panel and I like homebrews.

We'll talk about the origins of flavor in malt beverages — ale, stout, porter — and not strictly beer. Always, the final criteria on your beer is taste. You could have all the analysis in the world done, but your final exam is a taste test. At Siebel we have ten taste panelists. Each has a private booth, and we drink from rose-colored glasses so the color and foam does not influence our judgment. We mark down our impressions, and when everyone has finished, we unveil the beer, identify it and talk about it.

What we want to do is understand normal and abnormal flavors, what causes them and what corrective action we can take for off-flavors. To do this we'll adhere to the following outline.

1. Esters
2. Volatile phenols (these are very important)
3. Fatty acids
4. Diacetyl
5. Sulfur compounds
6. Grainy, harsh
7. Moldy, musty, earthy
8. Oxidation
9. Metallic
10. Microbial spoilage

ESTERS

There are at least ninety esters identified in beer. Synonyms for esters are vinous and winy which are very aromatic-type, positive flavors. In beer, esters are a product of organic acids and alcohol. They are formed within the yeast cell with the yeast enzymes. The ester with the highest concentration is ethyl acetate, which is formed from ethyl alcohol and acetic acid. Isoamyl acetate can be tasted at 2 ppm, but it can vary in the beer depending on how the beer is manufactured and fermented.

	Range	Taste Threshold
Ethyl acetate	7 - 48	30 ppm
Isoamyl acetate	0.8 - 6.6	2
2-phenyl	0.1 - 1.5	3
Ethyl captyl	0.08 - 1.4	1
Isobutyl	0.03 - 1.2	1
Methyl formate	0.37	—

Initial Taste Profile

J.E. SIEBEL SONS' COMPANY, INC.

Lab No.: 9999999
Identity: ABC Lager Beer
Package type: 12 oz. Amber One Way Bottle
Packaging date: Aug. 23, 1985

		Average
Stale <———Oxidation———>Fresh	xxxxxxxxx	I-9 IU
Thin <———Body———->Full		I** 2 IU
Less <———Flavorful———>More	***	I-3 IU
Harsh <———Palate———>Smooth	***	I-3 IU
Low <———Hop Intensity—->High		I 0 IU

AROMATIC, winy	I************** 15 IU, 9 Panelists
Fruity, estery	I****** 6 IU, 4
Spicy	I* 1 IU, 1
Aley	I
Alcoholic	I**2 IU, 1

BITTER, (non-hop)	I******************* 20 IU, 9
Malty	I********* 9 IU, 6
Caramel	I
Syrupy	I

DRY	I********** IU, 7
Astringent	I*************** 16 IU, 7
Husk, grainy	I************** 14 IU, 7
Worty	I* 1 IU, 1
Sulfitic (SO$_2$)	I** 2 IU, 2
Sulfidic (R-SH)	I* 1 IU, 1

YEASTY	I

DMS	Ixx 2 IU, 1
Lightstruck, skunky	I
Musty, cellar	Ixxx 3 IU, 1
Cardboard, paper	Ixxx 3 IU, 2
Burnt, scorched	Ixxxx 4 IU, 2
Bready, overpasteurized	Ixxxxxxxx 8 IU, 5
Termo/spoiled wort	Ixxx 3 IU, 2
Diacetyl	Ixxxxxxxx 8 IU, 5
Acidic, tart	Ixxxxxxxxxx 10 IU, 4
Metallic	I
Medicinal, phenolic	I
Foreign, off	Ixx 2 IU, 2

(Code: * are desirable and x are undesirable). Panel rating: -1.6

Comments: Diacetyl odor and taste, Very oxidized. Light on flavor and harsh. Very grainy and astringent, rather bacterial and dry. Poor appeal.

Printed with permission from Ted Konis.

The formation of esters depends on the yeast strain. Some strains produce more esters, others less. The second factor is temperature. The higher the fermentation temperature, the more ester formation. Of course this holds true for malt liquors as they are fermented at warmer temperatures, so consequently there is more ester formation.

The third is the tight-pot fermentation. There is more ester formation in a stirred fermentation, which takes about three days or a continuous fermentation system, which takes about two and a half days. Twenty years ago when I was with Carling Brewing in Fort Worth, Texas, we had continuous fermenting and continuous brewing. We couldn't match the regular product because of higher ester fermentation.

SUMMARY OF FERMENTATION FLAVORS

			Low growth:
			More ester,
Air —>			sweeter,
Yeast concentrate —>		**Yeast**	higher pH
Malt content —>		**Growth**	*High growth:*
Lipids —>			dry, tarter,
			sulfury

High-pitching rates also have high esters. High-gravity brewing produces more esters even after the beer is diluted. Aerating at the start of fermentation also causes more ester formation. The English were very reluctant to go into high-gravity brewing because of the high ester concentration in the beer. Instead, they tried to restrict the growth of yeast and aerate at the end to suppress ester formation.

The pH effect is not terribly influential on ester formation. If you add lipids or fatty acids, you get more ester formation. You can do this easily: experiment by taking the squeezings from your spent grains, which are high in lipids and fatty acids. You will find that you get a faster fermentation and more esters. But I don't recommend this as a procedure because it can lead to oxidative flavors.

VOLATILE PHENOLS/SOURCES

Volatile phenols are such an important factor that their presence could be the kiss of death for your brewery. Phenols in beer come from malt and hops. Tannins and antocyanigens fall into that class of phenols. Normally there are from 15 to 30 ppm total volatile phenols in American beers. An analysis we did on six national shippers showed about 22 ppm. These give the beer a little snap and aren't unpleasant.

But when there is an excessive amount, it causes an off-flavor. At 80 ppm, it is objectionable. The flavor is described as medicinal, herbal, spicy, clovelike, band-aid and smoky.

When I suspect phenol, I don't ask for analysis. That costs about $200 and takes most of the day to run. And then if the result is, "Phenols, 30 ppm," what does that tell me? Nothing! The reason is that the beer could also have 3 ppb chlorophenol which will indicate another kind of problem. I ask for a blind taste test.

One sample to which I added phenol at 120 ppm (the threshold for taste is about 80 ppm) was tasted by our panel. The taste panel of ten has two members who can't taste phenol. Everyone else runs to the sink to spit it out except those two — they love it. Genetically, they don't have the capacity to taste phenol. What happens to a brewmaster who isn't sensitive to phenol? He or she must recognize that and depend on someone else to taste it.

If there is a phenol taste in a beer, the consumer will not touch it again. And believe me, it takes one generation for a brewer to regain self-respect.

One source for phenol is water with a high phenol content due to industrial waste. Steam condensate is another source. It is wise not to use live steam to heat your cooker or your mash mixer, because your steam may be treated with phenolic substances, lignins or amines. Under high temperatures and pressures, these can turn into volatile phenols. Even a brewery with a closed system could develop a leak whereby live steam could enter the product.

I've done a lot of work on this with suppliers of boiler treatments. They excuse the potential problem by saying, "Our boiler treatment compounds are FDA approved." True, phenol won't kill you — but it may kill your brewery. The best thing is to use boiler compounds that do not contain phenol or phenol-producing agents.

Cleaning compounds are another source of phenol. When cleaning tanks or vessels, make sure they are well rinsed. Chlorine is in cleaning compounds, and the taste threshold for chlorophenol is 1 to 3 ppb. It is very, very potent.

The next source of phenol is yeast. We know this: some wine and wild yeasts produce phenol, so yeast must be pure. Even if a small percentage of wild yeast enters a culture, it will take over and produce phenol or other off-flavors because it is very viable.

Some bacteria produce phenol, especially wort spoilage organisms. Bacteria may enter mash that is left sitting overnight. I've come across two instances in which phenols were produced by bacteria. One large American brewer forgot to put yeast in the cool wort — and got phenol. In another case, a brewery in Central America called me to come down, and I immediately tasted phenol in the beer. After a plant inspection, we found that the lines to the wort starter vessel were completely dirty with bacteria. The processing heat didn't kill them; it just pushed them through into the wort.

Can and crown liner coatings cause phenol. You would think that, in this day and age, these would be immune from phenol production. But earlier this year, a crown manufacturer bought $1 million-worth of beer to pour down the drain. The liners contributed phenol to the beer.

Improperly cured phenolic-lined tanks is another source. The phenol coatings in water and beer tanks and processing vessels are inexpensive, but avoid them because they can impart phenol taste to the beer.

Diatomaceous earth can also contribute phenol. It may absorb off-flavors and odors, so make sure your filter-material is good. Another phenol source is slip sheets. Empty cans or bottles may have cardboard or plastic in between them. This material can impart phenolic-type flavors to the beer.

FATTY ACID FLAVORS

These are flavors that taste like lard; Anheuser-Busch calls them labox. They can occur due to autolyzed yeast and so they have an autolyzed taste. If the fermentation temperature is too warm, the yeast burst and release these fatty acids into the beer.

Crown liners are also a source for this fatty taste. To test for crown-liner phenol, we take draft beer, package it using a hand crowner, pasteurize it at 140 degrees F (60 degrees C) for ten minutes, then lay the container on its side. We taste it at zero days, seven and fourteen. Pasteurization enhances that fatty flavor.

DIACETYL

Diacetyl smells and tastes like rancid butter. When you go to New York and have kosher butter, you can taste the diacetyl. It's good in kosher butter, but not in beer. One source of diacetyl is specific yeast strains. Normally, diacetyl is produced and then the yeast reduce it. A specific yeast strain may not be able to sufficiently reduce diacetyl. "Petite" yeast cells, very small ones, usually do not reduce diacetyl well.

The higher the initial fermentation temperature, the more diacetyl is produced. Generally in the United States, the correct fermentation temperature is 45 to 50 degrees F (7 to 10 degrees C) for lagers and 65 to 68 degrees F (18.5 to 20 degrees C) for ales.

Yeast suspension at the end of fermentation is very important for proper diacetyl reduction. How does a brewer accomplish this? He or she reaches the apparent extract — say 2.50 — at which point fermentation is usually begun. Does the brewer then begin cooling? No. The fermentation is given an extra day to keep the yeast in suspension and reduce the diacetyl. Then it is cooled.

So, if you are using two fermentations, wait one extra day past the secondary before you cool your beer. Most of the diacetyl should be reduced because you held the yeast. It is very important not to rush fermentation.

And last of all, oxygen added during fermentation can raise the peak — not initially, but during fermentation. If you add air at the end of fermentation, you disturb the anaerobic cycle of the yeast, and it may not properly reduce diacetyl.

If you don't have enough amino acids in the wort, the yeast will drop out and not produce diacetyl. If you use all malt, no problem. If you use malt and syrup at a 50/50 ratio, you may be asking for trouble because you don't have enough amino acids to sustain life for yeast.

Wort pH is not that important. Low wort pH favors diacetyl production as does beer spoilage bacteria — pediococci and lactobacilli — which are also diacetyl producers.

SULFUR COMPOUNDS

A lot of importance is placed on sulfur compounds — the total SO_2 in beer. Malt contributes a little (0 to 100 ppm), there is very little from hops (up to several 100 ppm), and negligible amounts from corn or rice because they use SO_2 during the process. Most SO_2 is formed during fermentation by the yeast acting on the protein.

Most fresh American beers contain about 10 ppm SO_2. Our panel can taste it at about 15 ppm. The FDA now says that they might make that the top level and BATF will follow suit.

DMS, dimethyl sulfide, has a grainy, sweet, corn-type flavor. The taste threshold is about 85 ppb. DMS can come from malt, bacteria and yeast metabolism. The maltsters have cleaned up their act, and the malt is pretty good. I know one brewer, however, who uses high-moisture malt (12 percent), and he always has DMS in his beer because when the malt is kilned to drive off the moisture, the DMS precursors are driven off.

Light is a catalyst to flavor change. Amber bottles prevent skunky or lightstruck beer flavors for a few weeks. Green bottles, which give you a prestige package, protect the beer for a few days before it develops sunstruck flavors in the presence of sunlight or florescent light. Flint bottles protect for only a few hours. So if you want a good, stable product use amber bottles or cans.

GRAINY, HARSH, HUSK, ASTRINGENT, BITTER

Alkaline water, including sparge water, causes the grainy, husk flavors. Water with high sulfate content does also. Metals like iron and copper give the astringent taste — it is not hop bitterness. Iron should be limited to 0.15 ppm maximum, copper to 0.30 ppm maximum in brewing water.

Excess trub in the fermenter causes these harsh flavors. If hot break is pushed into the fermenter, it results in harsh, grainy characters. Too much tannic acid, if used, also gives harshness.

Poor kettle break gives harshness, as does a long runoff of the wort. If malt husks from the bottom of the bin are used, they contribute a grainy character. But this is easy to detect. If you're normally brewing at 11 OG, and the brewer at night makes a brew at 9 OG, maybe he or she is at the very bottom of the malt box.

When I was with Carling Brewery, our brewmaster in Tacoma, Washington, had the best efficiency, the best yield, but the poorest drinking beer. He got an A for efficiency and an F for drinking quality. What he did was to sparge the hot break in the hot wort tank and add that to his fermenter. He got the extract, but also the grainy, astringent character. You can't have both efficiency and good product.

Illustration by Vicki Hopewell

MUSTY, MOLDY, EARTHY

Where do these musty, moldy flavors come from? Years ago, they came from wooden tanks. Today, be careful of your water; algae can contribute to a musty character. Brewers should taste their beer, of course; but they should also taste their incoming water for phenol and mustiness.

These flavors also come from mold growth. Open fermenters in the cellar may result in this character. Beer hoses are another source. If they are cracking, they have areas for mold growth. You should clean your water-holding tanks every six months to prevent these off-flavors.

Clean your sand/carbon/gravel filters, too. Periodically backwash them with steam. Smell your water hoses. Are they musty? Infrequently, fermenters may also contribute to this flavor. A rule of thumb is this: if you clean and sanitize a tank and don't use it for one week, sanitize it again to make it fresh smelling.

Musty flavors intensify with age and oxidation. You cannot filter out these characteristics. Activated carbon won't do a thing because it is not that selective. This is also true with total, volatile phenols. That's why prebrewing checks are so important. Stroh Brewing Company and also Schlitz Breweries use diatomaceous earth filters with carbon on all incoming plant water. That's expensive, but they want to make certain that nothing gets in.

OXIDATION

Oxidation gives cardboardy, papery, woody-type flavors. The taste threshold is 70 ppm. This is the stale-agent flavor that happens when we introduce air into beer after fermentation.

To decrease chances of oxidation, watch vessel headspace. When a tank is filled, it needs CO_2 counterpressure. Not everyone can afford that, however, so the next solution is having antivortex devices intact. When beer comes into a tank, it geysers before it settles down, which exposes it to air. These antivortex devices are little baffles that spread the beer more evenly on entry.

Another point to follow is good brewing technique. If filling two vessels and one is almost full, crack the valve to begin filling the other. When the full one is 85 to 90 percent full (with headspace), close the valve to it and open the other one wide for gentle filling.

Likewise, if a tank is sucked dry during emptying, a vortex is created, which also sucks in air. The solution is to move the beer slowly, just cracking the valve so that it comes down gently.

If you're adding filter aids, stabilizers, primings, finings or post-fermentation hops, try to add them without adding air. Some brewers mix the addition with CO_2 and push it into the beer that way so as not to add air.

The third point is cellar procedures. Centrifuges are now hermetically sealed, but still the brewer must be careful not to pick up air. When you change over in packaging, you can pick up air, as also happens in startup and shutdown. The biggest faults in plants are pump seals. If there isn't a good seal when beer is being pumped, it sucks air and oxidation begins. One way to tell if pump seals are good is to test for leaks with a compound gauge. If the gauge shows negative, a vacuum is being created and air is being sucked in and is hurting your beer.

What can you do if there's air in your beer? One solution is purging, but I don't like this method. You run the carbonating stones in the tank and the foam comes out the top. You are driving off the air and replacing it with CO_2, but the dissolved oxygen is already in there doing its damage. You're driving off most of the nitrogen — and some oxygen — and at the same time, you're handling the beer roughly, which causes head loss.

Also, the nice foam constituents of that beer are being discarded, which means loss of some of the isoalpha acids concentrated in the foam. If you analyzed a beer and its foam for isoalpha acids, you'd find that the foam has a great many more. The carbonating stone air purge method should be a last-ditch measure.

Many brewers use antioxidant such as potassium metabisulfite and sodium metabisulfite at 30 ppm or one to one-and-a-half pounds per 100 barrels. But many brewers are switching to ascorbic acid or ascorbates as reducing agents.

METALLIC FLAVORS

When you pick up iron or copper flavors in your beer, be concerned about the process after the kettle. Most iron and copper are deposited in the hot break. Usually iron can be tasted in amounts greater than 0.15 ppm and copper can be tasted in amounts greater than 0.30 ppm.

When I was a brewmaster at our plant in Cleveland, we always ran Red Cap Ale first thing Monday morning, and it was always high in copper — 0.40 ppm. We checked it out and found that every weekend the lines were cleaned with caustic, using a little phosphoric acid. They were then rinsed and deemed ready for packaging. But when I ran the ale, it picked up the copper from the clean lines.

What can be done to prevent this? The copper must be passivated. Before the lines were cleaned, the copper had oxidized, which prevented the beer or ale from picking up the copper. But when the lines were cleaned with caustic, the oxide layer was removed. To solve this problem, we passivated with sodium citrate in a 1 percent solution — followed by thorough rinsing — to oxidize the copper.

MICROBIAL SPOILAGE

The key to preventing spoilage is starting fermentation as soon as possible after the wort is cool thus minimizing potential for infection. As soon as the yeast is pitched, the pH drops, the alcohol begins to form and CO_2 creates an anaerobic environment in which many of these bacteria cannot work. So pitch as soon as possible after the cooling wort to prevent DMS and diacetyl.

Acetic acid formation is a problem when using wooden fermenters. But it can be overcome by filling the tank with 200 ppm chlorinated solution after the tank has been scrubbed. Then, before the yeasted wort comes in, drop it to another tank. That's the only way I know of to clean wooden tanks.

With this information, you should be able to prevent many off-flavors, or at least recognize their sources if you do get them.

SPOILAGE ORGANISMS IN WORT

Site	Flavor	Organism
wort — early fermentation	phenolic sulfury, DMS	E. aerigebes klebsiella
wort — early fermentation	DMS, diacetyl	H. protea
wort — fermentation	diacetyl, lactic acid	Pediococcus Lactobacillus
wort — cask	acetic acid	acetobacter
process — bright beer	apples/acetic acid	gluconobacter acetonones
process — bright beer	bad apples/H_2S	zynomonas
fermenter dilution process, filling	herbal/phenolic/ musty/moldy	wild yeast mold, bacteria algae

FLAVOR PROFILES

ILSE SHELTON

eer flavor is such an interesting subject. Even though the topic has been studied for many, many years, we are just at the beginning. In this chapter, I want to guide you from the basics of tasting to what I consider typical beer flavors.

During the past fifty years, a tremendous amount of research into beer flavors has been done, and it might seem that we would be able to put an end to the "art of brewing" and formulate beer scientifically. You can measure the components of a beer with very expensive, analytical tools and obtain a graph that represents your beer's flavor. You can have two different beers chemically analyzed, and when the data from each is compared, the beers seem to be identical. Yet if you taste them, you find they do not taste the same. As a taster, you too are being used as an analytical instrument. Tasting is the one area where you cannot be out-performed by the most expensive analytical tool. Your nose, your taste, and your knowledge give the final result.

At Siebel Institute of Technology, part of the curriculum includes daily tasting sessions to familiarize our students with different beer flavors. It's always amazing to me that even though most students have been involved in brewing for a long time — and they have heard about certain off-flavors such as diacetyl, DMS, and skunkiness — they really don't understand what tasting is all about and want to learn more. I start by asking, "What is flavor?" Originally it was assumed that flavor arose from aroma — the volatiles — and the taste. But recently a third category has come into play: the feeling or trigeminal sensation.

To begin, what do you know about olfactory sensations? You undoubtedly know that aromatics

involve your nose, but are you aware of the process when you smell something? At the first sniff of a beer, many aromatic molecules enter your nose, passing by very fine, hair-like sensors inside you nose that record the first impression and transmit it to your brain. Now, remember, this is a first impression. How do you taste beer? Do you slug it down or sniff it first and then taste it? You must take your time, or you never really pick up the aroma and/or taste. Take one sniff, inhale through your nose, and then start analyzing. This makes use of your olfactory senses to process the aromatics. The nose has an alarm system that closes the olfactory sense down when a smell is overpowering. For example, if you smell a little bit of ammonia, you detect it at first, then you can't smell anything. You have become over-saturated, unable to identify the compound. The same is true when there are a lot of other aromas such as hand lotion, hair-spray, perfume, or after-shave in your environment when you are tasting beer. When you are tasting, these odors confuse your brain into making a completely wrong analysis.

People sometimes tell me they can't smell aromas. My experience is that everyone can smell but they haven't allowed themselves to really study the different components and do not recognize them. Or they haven't given themselves sufficient time to relax. There are no actual cases of anosmia, that is, the inability to smell. There are recorded cases of not being able to smell specific odors.

The second category in analyzing beer flavors is the gustatory sensation. Just as your nose senses aromas, your tongue senses the basic tastes of salty, sour, sweet, and bitter. The tongue is a wonderful tool for analyzing flavors once you familiarize yourself with where on your tongue you pick up different taste sensations. For instance, the very tip of your tongue senses sweetness. The sides of your tongue sense saltiness and sourness. And in the very back are the sensors for bitterness. There are thicker layers of skin in the back of the tongue under which the bitterness stimuli are located, so bitter flavor chemical components have a tougher time penetrating those senses and the bitter flavor lingers on. That can be undesirable when a beer is very powerfully, strongly bitter, for example of 40 to 50 bitterness units. It tends to mask all other flavors.

When tasting, a prudent taster takes one or two very small sips, then sets the glass down and tries to recognize the most intense flavors. Don't oversaturate your senses; you must allow yourself at least twenty seconds before you repeat the process and assure yourself that a flavor is indeed one you recognize. This is where most people make a mistake; they rush from taste to taste, never allowing themselves the time to readapt, which is what it is called. When you are tasting, your brain can analyze only about eight to ten attributes before it gets extremely confused.

Finally, the third sensation in analyzing beer flavors is the trigeminal sensation. Only in the last ten to fifteen years has this sensation been deemed important. The olfactory and gustatory sensations are chemical, but the trigeminal sensation is a physical sensation, a tactile sensation. The trigeminal nerve lies along the side of your cheek and picks up sensations in the lower and upper gums and sends a message to your brain. I'm sure you have all smelled vinegar and then felt a clenching sensation in your cheek just below your ear. That is a trigeminal sensation.

In beer, the long-lasting, warm feeling from the alcohol is a trigeminal sensation. A lot of researchers believe that this taste sensation enhances your perception of other flavors. The body and fullness of a beer are definitely trigeminal sensations, and I believe they too enhance flavor by giving it smoothness and balance.

There are a lot of different flavor terminologies for beer, and these have been organized into a flavor wheel. The flavor wheel categorizes flavors into classes and subclasses. For instance, classes include mouthfeel, fullness, aromatics, and sulfury. Let's say you taste a beer and recognize a sulfury sensation. But what is the sulfur compound? Is it yeastiness or skunkiness that can indicate a problem beer? You taste the beer again, and then look on the flavor wheel for the subcategory of sulfury. Is it the sulfury taste of cooked vegetables that signals DMS? Is it the sulfury taste of rotten eggs or the sulfur smell of a burned match? A highly sulfidic taste is undesirable, but some people like just a slight bit of sulfur in a beer. This is why you should work with the flavor wheel. Taste a beer and try to identify an ester or an aromatic and then study the flavor wheel to see what particular compound is present in the subcategory.

There are some terms in beer flavor terminology that are used frequently and with which you should be familiar. Fruity is one. It is broken down into subcategories such as citrus and banana. Fruitiness in beer is a slight reminiscence of an apple flavor. Another key term is hoppy, its flavor being the result of aromatic hop constituents. Sniff the beer and let the aroma penetrate your nose. Hops should give a pleasant smell, or if not, the hops may be stale. Another term is bitter, which derives from hops and is the key component in beer. Paul Shipman said that beer-making was at the roots of our civilization. I think he's completely right. Since people could not drink the water and survive, someone had to come up with something that would fight the bacteria. That was hops, and the accompanying bitterness. The components of bitterness in an extremely high concentration can act as an antibacterial, and I believe that ancient beers were highly bitter.

Maltiness is a key flavor in beer. It can also impart minute traces of DMS, eighty to 100 ppb. The phrases "lingering bitterness" or "afterbitter" are terms used to describe the lasting effect of higher bitterness units. Tart is a sensation caused by acid, and while it's pleasant in minute amounts, it's very harsh and astringent in higher amounts. Oxidized is a stale, papery flavor that no one wants in beer, but which occurs — especially if anti-oxidants aren't used. I have noticed that a lot of micro-brewed beers, which are often high-malt beers, do not exhibit oxidation compounds as quickly as the light beers. Possibly, the papery compound is being masked by the greater amounts of ester produced by the greater amount of malt. At its onset, oxidation in a high-malt brew is more a fruitiness and an astringency. It seems to taste more like acetic acid. Personally, I like it because it is a little more fruity. But when it gets beyond that, and the paperiness sets in, then a high-malt beer can have a very stale, cardboardlike taste and a graininess.

A grainlike smell can be observed when cereal is cooked for a long time. The aromatics in the atmosphere are called grainy.

Phenolic compounds are unwanted in beer, especially the chlorophenol ones. Their flavor is reminiscent of bleach and disinfecting chemicals. Some of them create a clovelike, spicy character that characterizes a Weiss beer.

Skunkiness can be produced within twenty minutes if beer is left in sunlight in a clear bottle. It occurs very quickly and is very unpleasant.

Bacteria produce a large group of different flavors. Some of them are musty, grainy, vinegary, and celerylike. If a brewer detects these aromas, he or she should be alerted to the possibility of bacterial infection.

Yeasty is another category on the flavor wheel. What this basically means is that the protein in the yeast has broken down. It smells like beef or chicken soup. To me it smells like the B vitamins because minute traces of vitamin B are present in yeast.

Diacetyl produces a butterlike flavor although I associate it with the taste of caramel candy or popcorn. Usually, it has lactic, dairy flavor notes. It imparts a smoothness to a beer, a nice feeling. The detection level by humans can be as low as sixty parts per billion. In a lot of European beers, a little diacetyl is preferred by beer drinkers and is only rejected by the brewmaster or someone with knowledge of brewing and fermentation.

Finally, mouthfeel is important in a beer. I like to drink a microbrewed beer because it gives me mouthfeel and body, something light and nonalcoholic beers are missing. These attributes are feeling sensations that the trigeminal nerve is responsible for and are very difficult to describe. They are flavors a product taster has to learn to recognize. Higher amounts of dextrins in a beer result in mouthfeel and make the beer taste thicker.

The following test is the best example of mouthfeel. Taste a light beer — or even better an ultra-light beer — and experience the thinness of the beverage. It is reminiscent of water. Then get a malt liquor and experience the difference — the fullness and the roundness. That is mouthfeel.

To what intensity should flavor components be present in beer? We must differentiate between very intense, less intense, and least intense. A typical American lager has basically three major flavor components: bitter, alcoholic, and carbonation. Microbrewed beers, on the other hand, have as primary flavors the additional components maltiness, esteriness, and sweetness. However, taken together, the secondary components probably make up the major part of the beer's flavor impact. In the order of flavor activity, one often finds the hop aroma compounds first, then perhaps malt and caramel notes, especially in dark beers. In a pale beer of low hop rate, the various fermentation esters come first. Among those we find the bananalike esters, acetates, and fusel alcohols. Ethyl acetate with its solventlike flavor is quite distinct.

If you weight any of these components as a primary flavor note, you can get a different beer. For example, if esters become a primary flavor component, then you have a malt liquor. Some breweries do very well with beers that have a trace amount of DMS. Cheesy flavors, such as isovaleric and caprylic, are primary flavor notes in some English beers and vinegary acids are very pronounced in Belgian lambics.

When you look at a flavor wheel, the question becomes, how can I train myself or my flavor panel to taste various flavors? At Siebel, we have devised a profile for tasting a beer based on the work of Dr. Joem Oehlhausen. We have seven beers that have to be rated. This is a large number and only an expert taster can taste that many beers. However, on one side, you rate the different beers according to their positive attributes and on the other side, you rate them according to their negative attributes.

For example, let's start with oxidation. First, tasters rate the beer as having less or more oxidation. Then the beer is rated on smoothness, hoppiness, yeastiness, and so on. These flavors are basically positive. Then we move from DMS down to foreign flavors we consider negative — which we don't want present in a beer. When it comes down to the final rating, if you have not found anything in the negative column, you cannot give a negative rating — even if you don't like the beer. That's because, according to the flavor components, it is an acceptable beer. You rate the beer from zero to plus four and zero to minus four. It is human nature to not rate a beer a plus four, people are always looking for one better.

This profile is a very complex, descriptive analysis report. You, the taster, are not asked a preference, rather you are asked to analyze with your senses. You are used as an instrument that has to be tuned and calibrated every day.

When I consider the German beers coming into North America, I know that I want to drink only beers brewed here. I would not drink an imported beer here for a variety of reasons. When I look at the beers in North America, I rate the beers from large breweries as being like McDonald's. They serve a purpose. When I am hungry, I can eat. I know what to expect, and it never changes. The quality is there, yet if I want to taste a beer different in character — different in certain attributes — then it is the local microbrewery that serves me. Because of that, I think microbreweries — with their beers' unique styles and unique flavors — have a lot to give to the North American beer taster.

TRAINING OURSELVES IN FLAVOR PERCEPTION AND TASTING

RAOUL PALAMAND, PH.D.

Beer flavor is a subject very close to my heart, as it should be for anyone interested in deriving the maximum enjoyment from the art and science of producing and consuming this great product — beer. I'm going to cover some fairly basic things about tasting, sensory perceptions and beer flavor that can be applied by homebrewers, commercial brewers or simply people who enjoy drinking beer.

Flavor is one of the most important aspects of foods and beverages, and in fact, it is fair to say that flavor is the most important aspect of beer, because beer is consumed not for its alcohol content, but for its refreshing flavor. Let's start with the definition of beer flavor. Flavor is described as a complex sensation comprising odor, taste, and mouthfeel factors, which refer to the texture and temperature. In other words, you can consider flavor a combined sensation of aroma, taste, and feeling factors.

FLAVOR

Aroma — Fruity, floral, alcohol, spicy, resinous, sulfide, etc.

Taste — Sweet, sour, salty, bitter, alkaline, metallic

Feeling — Hot, cold, drying, harsh, smooth, astringent

To expand on that, the five components of flavor are taste, aroma, appearance, mouthfeel, and sound. Appearance and sound are very important. A beer colored blue might not taste as good as one with normal color, although it may have all the other flavor aspects. Consider sound. Soggy celery or potato chips don't taste good — they should be crunchy.

Beer is brewed to provide the consumer with a pleasing flavor, a refreshing effect, a thirst-quenching property, a pleasing appearance, and excellent drinkability. It is brewed under certain controlled conditions to produce certain flavors.

Briefly, let's look at the localization of the sensory receptors and their application to tasting beer. The sensors for aroma are located in the nose in the olfactory cleft near the olfactory brain. The ability to notice odors is a primal sense. The taster should be in an odor-free room, he or she shouldn't be wearing aftershave, cologne or perfume, and there should be no smoking during tasting.

Taste sensors are distributed all over the mouth parts, and not just on the tongue. Most of the time, we think of taste as being on the tongue, but with the upper palate you can taste sweet, salt, sour, and bitter. There are even taste buds down the throat. For the most accurate tasting experience, avoid spicy foods, gum or mouth washes prior to the tasting.

In tasting beer it is important to be aware of taste bud locations because as the beer goes past the back of the tongue and on down the throat, we perceive the flavors of the beer beyond those detected by the tongue.

The sample to be tasted should be poured at about 40 degrees F (4.5

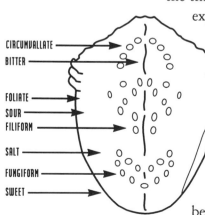

CIRCUMVALLATE
BITTER
FOLIATE
SOUR
FILIFORM
SALT
FUNGIFORM
SWEET

degrees C) into clean, polished glasses, with or without foam. Tasting is where you derive the most information per unit of liquid consumed. In analyzing beer flavor, you take a sip of beer and make sure it covers all the areas in the mouth to get the full appreciation of what the beer has to offer.

As far as odor, the olfactorium is lined with pinnacle structures known as olfactory cells, supported on either side by epithelial cells. The olfactory cells end in fine, hairlike projections called olfactory cilia. It is here the chemicals are received and passed on to the olfactory brain for interpretation. There are ten million receptor cells in one person, and we can theoretically detect more than sixteen million different odors. In terms of detecting odor, take short, rabbit sniffs rather than one long one. The olfactory cells have a tremendous capacity to renew themselves very quickly and by taking short sniffs, you are subjecting your olfactory senses to the same, repeated signal. This allows you to pick out what the flavor compounds are. The epithelial cells, besides providing support, also secrete mucous to keep the cells moist. The mucous tends to thicken when you have a head cold, partially immobilizing the cells. This is the reason why a person with a head cold can't smell or taste effectively.

On the tongue, there are tiny projections called papillae, of which there are four types: fungiform, filiform, foliate and circumvallate. In carnivorous animals, filiform do not participate in tasting and

OLFACTORY BRAIN

OLFACTORY CLEFT

SWEET
SALT
SWEET
SALT
SOUR
BITTER
BITTER
SOUR
SALT
SWEET
BITTER
SOUR

are used to lick meat off of bones. Foliate are not developed in humans. We use the circumvallate and fungiform papillae, which contain the taste buds, for sensing taste sensations.

The circumvallate papillae at the back of the tongue resemble a mound surrounded by a moat. The taste buds are located in the moats. Taste sensations are perceived more at the back of the tongue, and the liquid must go down in the moat to interact with the taste buds. The carbon dioxide in beer has two functions: It pushes the liquid into those moats, and by its acidic nature, carbon dioxide helps to clean out the bitterness. If you ever taste flat beer, you'll find a bitter, lingering taste.

The taste buds resemble flowers in shape, hence the name, and consist of the taste cells and support cells. The taste cells transmit information to the brain where it is interpreted as taste. As you know, in the case of olfaction, the stimulation is almost instantaneous. But it takes longer for us to react to taste compounds.

Taste buds are concentrated on different areas of the tongue. Humans have about nine thousand taste buds, and we can recognize four basic tastes and at least eight other chemicals. Sweet is tasted on the tip of the tongue, salt on the front sides, sour on the middle sides, and bitter on the back. This is not to say that we don't taste in the center, but in certain other areas the cells are concentrated, causing a higher level of taste impression.

When tasting, sip no more than a tablespoonful and slosh it around your mouth, letting the liquid contact the taste buds and the upper palate, then back near the throat. In this way, you get the most information. You don't have to drink a half glass of beer. With two or three sips, you have subjected your taste buds to the maximum sensation.

With the first, you record the character. With the second, you judge the sweet, sour, and bitter tastes, the order in which they occur. With the third sip, you determine the mouthfeel. Is it harsh, drying, astringent? With the fourth sip, you can know something about the aftertaste. Unlike with wine, the aftertaste in beer is a quick cutoff.

Let the beer go down your throat. Here, the bitter taste is the most predominant. Hop compounds produce the snappy, bitter taste we have all learned to love. But the peptic bitterness – that produced by the peptides, amino acids, proteins – tends to linger and is not very desirable. Hops neutralize peptic bitterness and that is why hops are preferable.

By looking at beer flavor and its sources we can determine how much attention is needed for each individual material in the beer in order to derive maximum flavor. The fermentation of malt and other cereal carbohydrates by yeast is the major source of beer flavor; in fact, the by-products of fermentation comprise what is known as beer flavor. In addition, raw material flavors — barley malt, adjuncts, and hops — affect flavor by direct contribution with little or no change.

You also have flavors derived from the brewhouse processes — kettle boiling and mashing. The mashing produces fermentable sugars, and, in the meantime, the proteins are hydrolyzed into amino acids and the amino acids act as flavor precursors in the kettle to produce the aroma compounds, the diketones and the caramels, etc. Kettle boiling also produces flavor compounds that act as anti-oxidants during later stages of beermaking.

Let's take a look at the composition of any beer. — Carbohydrates and proteins provide the foundation on which the flavor is built.

Typical Composition of Beer

Component	%	Chemicals	Function Major	Minor
Water	91.0	1	Flavor	
Ethanol	3.7	1	Flavor	Feeling Sens.
Carbohydrate	4.1	15	Mouthfeel	
Nitrogenous Matter (Prot.)	0.3	35	Foam	Mouthfeel
Ash	0.2	10	Flavor	Mouthfeel
Acids	0.1	3	Flavor	
CO_2	0.5	1		Mouthfeel
Others	0.1	800	Flavor	

— A good product has the best balance between the foundation and the flavoring compounds.

— Every product needs a minimum amount of flavor base for supporting its top flavor notes. Some light beers suffer from a lack of sufficient flavor base.

The constituents listed are what I call the beer flavor essence. They make one beer different from another.

Without a strong foundation, all the flavors jump out at you at one time, and there is no slow release of flavors as you sip beer. You want beer flavor to last until the last drop in the glass. That value is achieved only when you have a right proportion of the foundation to the taste and top flavor notes.

The type of chemical compounds represented by beer flavor essence are the higher alcohols, esters, fusel oil fractions, organic acids, carbonyl compounds, sulfur compounds, sulfur-containing carbonyl compounds, sulfur-containing acids, amines, amino carbonyls, hydrocarbons, and others. Every product needs a minimum amount of flavor foundation to support its flavor notes.

Following is a list of chemical classes of compounds present in the "other minor constituents" of beer.

CHEMICAL COMPOSITION OF BEER FLAVOR

Esters
Alcohols
Carbonyl Compounds
Sulfur Compounds
Amines
Amino Carbonyls

Thioesters
Thio Carbonyls
Thioacids
Organic Acids
Hydrocarbons

When you take a sip of beer do you really detect these flavor chemicals? Actually, they interact to produce a flavor sensation. When you get a fruity taste, a number of compounds are responsible. If you change the balance, you will not get the fruity esters.

Esters are abundantly found in nature in fruits and flowers. Carbonyl compounds, for example, diacetyl and 2.3 Pentanedione, give the buttery, nutty flavors. Organic acids produce fruity, buttery, cheesy flavors.

While glycerol is not very volatile, you can taste it in beer in levels of 1,000 to 2,000 ppm. It is sweet and smooth and also contributes to the body of beer. Hop acids produce the typical bitter taste of beer that we enjoy. Sulfur volatiles include a number of compounds that produce what we call a yeasty, starting cellar-type aroma. Polyphenols produce the astringency, the mouth-puckering sensation that can be readily detected in beer. Nitrogenous compounds produce mouthfeel and foam. Fusel alcohols, which is a term used for higher alcohols and esters, produce a typical fermentation aroma that is common to most fermented products, including wine and whiskey.

Hydrocarbons produce a citrus, green, hoppy aroma. Years ago we thought that none of the hop aroma constituents ever got into beer, but there is considerable evidence to show that hydrocarbons are present in beer and contribute to hoppy and citrusy aroma. Then there are miscellaneous polyfunctional compounds that are hard to describe, but they say beer.

A beer brewed under optimum conditions possesses a blend of flavors contributed to some extent by direct transfer of the characteristic flavors from raw materials, barley malt, cereal adjuncts, water, and hops, and to a much larger extent by various chemical and biochemical reactions involving these materials during the mashing, kettle boiling, fermentation, and cellar finishing operations.

MAJOR FLAVOR CONSTITUENTS

Ethanol and higher alcohols and esters produce many of the characteristics of beer. Major alcohol or ethyl alcohol, which is produced by enzymatic reduction of acetaldehyde formed from maltose, contributes a very apparent flavor property. This is the tongue-warming effect, or the slightly harsh flavor. Ethyl alcohol also helps to keep most of the beer compounds in solution. If you ever try to remove alcohol from a normally brewed beer, you get a certain amount of turbidity. That is because some of the solvent action of the alcohol is lost when you do this. Likewise, if you remove some of the esters, more flavor compounds go out of solution. Esters also function as solvents for other flavor constituents.

Higher alcohols, chiefly butyl and fusel alcohol, produce a typical, slightly pungent, sometimes throat-catching sensation. Phenyl ethyl alcohol, the major aromatic alcohol in beer, produces a floral, roselike character.

Esters are formed mainly by biosynthesis, and sometimes by chemicals. The esters are pleasant smelling compounds that help in blending flavors. They also act as solvents to keep flavors in solution that are not very soluble in water. Some of the flavors of esters are bananas, pineapple, and apples.

Chief sources for organic acids are amino acids. The long chain organic acids mainly affect taste, but when they are unsaturated, they more definitely affect taste aroma. They smell like paint or varnish, and break down into a whole bunch of undesirable flavor compounds producing papery, leathery, and cardboardy notes.

Carbonyl compounds are very important from the standpoint of flavor. They have low thresholds that produce a grainy, green hop character.

Diacetyl is sweet smelling, but also has a very low flavor threshold. Most of us have learned to dislike diacetyl in beer, and consider it a bad compound. Actually, at low levels, it produces a smoothing-out effect, and contributes positively to the overall flavor of beer. What we have to guard against is excessively high levels.

Metallic flavors were once thought to be produced only by metals such as iron, copper, etc., but we now know that under certain conditions unsaturated fatty acids of beer can break down into certain ketones that smell like rusty iron.

Sulfur compounds are produced by the action of yeasts on sulfur-containing amino acids. Sulfur compounds also are contributed by hops. They contribute flavoring compounds such as mercaptans — onion and garlic odors — and sulfides.

Hydrocarbons are derived mainly from hop essential oil fractions.

So, the many compounds present in beer represent a number of chemical classes. When you taste beer, a lot happens. We do not perceive all the individual flavors of the compounds. What happens is they are perceived as several integrated flavor notes. You might say the beer is hoppy, sweet, floral, grainy, and malty. You get the typical attractive quality of CO_2 as a gentle, faint sensation that carries sweet, sour, and bitter compounds. Then there are also the flavor and aroma characters such as estery, grainy, and yeasty.

These beer flavors derive from a number of sources. They derive from the raw materials, which are direct contributors of flavors such as malty, nutty, citrus, floral, and leafy notes.

As barley is malted, flavor compounds are produced that have a vegetable character, the leafy, green, and cucumberlike flavors. Then when the malt is kilned, toasted, grainy characters may be produced along with dimethyl sulfide, which has a cornlike or cabbagelike aroma, as well as the typical malty character.

Mashing, converting starch into fermentable sugar to provide food for the yeast, produces a host of flavor precursors that are converted into a variety of beer flavor notes at various stages of the brewing process.

Then hops are added to the sweet wort and boiled. Kettle boiling produces the heat-induced flavors. Hop aromatics are produced, along with bitter resins.

Up to this point, beer flavor depends on the quality of the raw materials. You can have a nice fermentation as long as plenty of sugars and nutrients are available for the yeast, but if you don't have good-quality materials you can get into trouble. Abnormal or poor-quality raw materials produce off-flavors even if you use a normal brewing process.

Beer is a dynamic system that constantly changes even after it is brewed. When you pasteurize, you only discourage the changes involved with the microbiological species, but the chemical changes continue to take place. In regard to aroma,

Typical Flavor Description of Fresh Beer

Aroma		Flavor (by mouth)	
Amplitude	1 - 1.5	Amplitude	1 - 1.5
Yeasty	0.5	CO_2	1.5
Fruity	1	Sweet	0.5 - 1
Alcohols	0.5	Estery	0.5 - 1
Grainy	1	Sour	1.5
Hops	‡	Grainy	1
		Yeasty	1
		Hops	0.5
		Bitter	1
		Astringent	0.5

Scale: 0 = none; ‡ = threshold; 1 = slight; 2 = moderate; 3 = strong

within one or two weeks of being made, beer begins to lose a little of its freshness, its amplitude. Let me explain amplitude. It has two aspects: you have to have the right compounds. You can have all the chemicals in the right balance, but without enough of them, you don't have the right amplitude. You can have plenty of flavor, but without one or two chemicals, you have decreased amplitude.

Can you communicate the flavor you are sensing to someone else? In the flavor business, too many chemists tend to use long terms to describe taste. Yet, if you say something tastes like stale milk powder, everyone knows what that is. Use terms that are familiar to people in reference to everyday products and experiences. Avoid chemical terms. Say, "It smells like freshly cut grass."

We all have the same kind of taste buds and olfactory cells; it is a matter of training yourself to recognize odors and tastes. Only a small percentage of people are taste and odor blind.

Avoid value judgments. People say, "It tastes good." That means nothing. Maybe you like cabbage and I don't. Avoid hedonics.

There are some special techniques for detecting beer tastes. Some people say they can't detect metallic, iron tastes, or drying tastes. Those taste centers are on the upper palate, so knowing this, take a small sip of beer to spread it over the tongue surface. Then press the tongue up against the upper palate. With this method, even low levels of metallic taste can be perceived. It allows you to taste the subthreshold properties.

The drying property is perceived at the front middle part of the tongue, back sides, and front upper arch. The drying property can best be described as almost like someone put fine sand in your beer. It is a little rough, gritty. To experience the drying sensation, take a sip of beer, flow it over the tongue, and then press the tongue against the front upper arch. You may even be able to taste the drying minerals in water this way.

To detect even minor flavor differences between samples, use the momentary adaptation technique. Take two glasses of beer that are only slightly dissimilar. Take a long whiff of one beer – not the rabbit sniffs – and then immediately smell the other. You will detect odors in the second beer that were not the same as those in the first. A lot of product duplication in the industry is done this way by trained people. The components are in so low concentration that analytical techniques don't detect them, but you can smell them.

How are desirable flavors produced? You need good raw materials and normal brewing process conditions with proper mashing, good, vigorous kettle boiling, critical control of time, pure, vigorous yeast, proper temperature, and appropriate oxygen levels. You can have normal brewing, but if one or more steps of the brewing process is abnormal, then you can get undesirable flavor character by generating off-flavor compounds, or by simply upsetting the balance. You may have a higher than desirable level of diacetyl, higher than desirable level of ketone, or any number of other flavor compounds. Beer flavor balance can be upset, and you get a totally undesirable flavor character.

One source of off-flavors is foreign materials such as contamination from metal or from plastics used in liners or hoses. These flavors enter the product through processing or packing steps and produce off-flavor compounds.

Most of these compounds that cause off-flavors are exceedingly potent. You don't need large concentrations of these to create flavor problems. Even at low levels, some of the compounds are readily noticeable. For example, cabbagy or sweet cornlike flavors are noticeable at 50 to 60 parts per billion of dimethyl sulfide. To put it into perspective, this would be equivalent to one minute of time in thirty years.

Catty odors or ribes, caused by air in the package, can be perceived at 55 parts per trillion level of the offending flavor chemical.

Skunky odor is produced at 1 to 2 parts of skunky perception per billion; cucumber at 500 parts of cucumber aldehyde per trillion; and buttery odor or diacetyl at 0.04 to 0.08 parts per million.

SOME UNDESIRABLE NOTES IN BEER AND THEIR CONTROL

Bready aromas are produced by high levels of acetaldehyde (20 to 25 ppm), a product of fermentation. To control this, control fermentation temperatures and make sure the yeast levels are up.

Burnt off-taste can be caused by malt kilning, or in some cases, molds or some fungi.

Buttermilky notes are fermentation derived, from lactic contamination or certain strains of yeast.

Buttery is caused mainly by diacetyl, and an adequate secondary fermentation can help to control this.

Butterscotch aroma is also caused by uncontrolled fermentation.

Cabbagy flavor occurs during kettle boil by dimethyl sulfide, which produces a cabbagelike or cornlike flavor. It can come from the malting process or contamination by certain microorganisms. To inhibit this, have adequate control of the malting process, use a vigorous kettle boil, and use only a pure yeast culture.

Cardboardy flavor is produced by warm storage of beer that promotes oxidation or the use of improperly cured cans. Sometimes even traces of certain oil compounds left in the can will produce cardboardy flavors. If you use cans in packaging beer, this is something to keep in mind.

Cheesy flavor is produced by using old hops or by warm storage of beer. So use fresh hops and store beer at cool temperatures.

Cucumber flavors or off-notes are produced from underkilning malt. The control for this is adequate kilning temperatures.

Drying sensations are caused from numerous compounds, but one precaution is to avoid celite residue in filtered beer.

Earthy flavors are often from mold contamination during malting or storage of malt. Control is in eliminating microbial contamination during the malting process.

Grapey flavor also is caused by oxidation. To minimize this, minimize the level of oxygen in the package, and store beer at cool temperatures.

Green or woody off-flavors are caused by long storage and improper handling of the product during storage.

Husklike characters are caused from long, warm storage of beer.

Leathery flavors are produced when old hops are used, and beer is subjected to warm storage for extended periods of time.

Malty flavors are caused in part by dimethyl sulfide, and a number of subtle compounds mainly produced by tainted malt. There are high levels of dimethyl sulfide precursors in malt, but a full, rolling boil can reduce the level of this compound.

Medicinal flavors result from contaminated water and contaminated malt. Chlorophenols may be formed when water contaminated with phenols is chlorinated to make it potable.

Metallic flavors may be derived by extracting iron from processing aids or by the formation of unsaturated ketones by breakdown of certain oils used in the can-making process. Cans are sometimes improperly coated or cured. To control this, avoid metal contamination from equipment surfaces and processing aids such as celite. Use clean metal and cans free of unsaturated fatty acids and carbonyls.

Musky off-odor can be produced by musty, stagnant water, which has algae growth. Malt also can produce this. Use good raw materials.

Nutty character can may from packing materials and can lubricants. The control is using clean cans free of contaminating lubricants.

Papery, again, is due to oxidation. Store beer at low temperature in the absence of oxygen and acidic contaminants.

Phenolic is caused by wild yeasts and bacterial contamination of water and cereals. To control this problem maintain a pure-culture yeast, and use quality raw materials.

Potatoey-type flavor can be caused by oxidation of beer.

Ribes or catty odors also are caused by oxidation during storage. Again, control headspace oxygen in the package.

Soapy characters are caused by a high level of fatty acids in beer and also the alkaline contamination of cleaning solution. Control is to rinse equipment thoroughly after cleaning.

Smoky flavors tend to come from a wild yeast contamination. Again, maintain pure yeast cultures.

Solventy flavors can come from unclean packaging materials. Ensure use of good packaging materials.

Stale grainy flavors are from oxidation. Store beer at low temperatures in the absence of oxygen.

Sunstruck, skunky flavors come from exposure of beer to light (sunlight or light containing harmful radiation of 350 to 700 nm). Of course, the control is to package beer in cans or dark amber bottles, but this off-flavor also may be controlled by treating hops to inactive sensitive agents.

Turpey is a term we use for the effect caused by old hops or storing beer at warm temperatures. Control is use fresh hops and store beer at low temperatures.

Winy flavors are caused by prolonged oxidation of beer, when beer has lost most of its beer flavor. Control is to store beer at low temperatures in the absence of oxygen.

The conclusion is that you can make good beer with good ingredients, good processes, and good packaging, but if storage conditions are not good, you can get numerous unfavorable reactions. Off flavors don't occur singly or doubly; they occur in multiples when storage is poor, when fermentation is poor, and when poor-quality raw materials are used.

You must be careful of taking risks in flavor. Your raw materials must be clean and of the right composition. With malts, do a chemical analysis to be sure of their quality, but also look at their color, condition, aroma, and taste.

Analyze to see that fatty acids aren't excessively high because they break down and produce some off-flavor compounds. Hops should have good aroma and a nice bouquet. Yeast should have purity of culture. Know what strain of yeast you are using and make sure it is healthy and well-maintained. Water — do a complete analysis, depending on the type of beer you want to make. In general, for any beer, you need to know the composition, the hardness, and other characteristics of the water.

Beer should be checked for the degree Plato to determine how well your process of fermentation is proceeding. Check CO_2 to make sure it is within the proper range; there is nothing worse than foamless, watery-looking beer.

Do these analyses, pay attention to raw materials, brewing processes, and storage conditions, and then work at becoming proficient in tasting beer.

A SIMPLE TECHNIQUE FOR EVALUATING BEER COLOR

GEORGE FIX, PH.D.

Color affects the appreciation and evaluation of beer in subtle but definite ways. The "halo effect" refers to a situation where a positive (or negative) response to one attribute leads to an overevaluation (or underevaluation) of other attributes. The color of beer can be a powerful but often subconscious generator of the "halo effect."

An example is the low marks given to otherwise satisfactory beers in competitions where the entry's color is inappropriate for the category. In professional tasting, the "halo effect" is generally regarded as an unacceptable bias. However, in less formal settings it reflects the natural influence that physical appearance of a food or beverage has over sensory anticipation. For this, and other reasons, color control in brewing is important, and the goal of this chapter is to review the basic issues.

Before describing the test we first review the units in which beer and wort color are measured, and then review the factors that affect color in malting and brewing.

COLOR UNITS
Beer and wort color traditionally have been measured visually, and early on the Lovibond (°L) scale was adopted as a standard. This consists of a

well-defined set of color samples that are used for comparison. A visual match with a beer or wort sample defines the °L of the sample. In modern brewing, photometric methods have replaced visual comparison, and the American Society of Brewing Chemists has developed the so-called Standard Reference Method (SRM), which is widely used. Results are expressed as degrees SRM, and for the purposes of this article these units can be regarded as the same as °L. Some examples are presented in the chart below.

Standard Reference Method (SRM) for Beer Color Evaluation

Basic Color	Hue	°L	Example	Degrees SRM
Yellow	light	0 - 2.5	Budweiser	= 2.0°
	pale	2.5 - 3.5	Average American Lager	= 2.5 - 3.9°
			Average German Pils	= 2.5 - 2.9°
	deep straw/ gold	3.5 - 5.5	Molson Export Ale	= 4.0°
			Gosser Spezial	= 4.0°
			Pilsener Urquel	= 4.2°
			Spaten Club Weiss	= 4.6°
Amber	light	5.5 - 10	Bass Pale Ale	= 10°
			Whitbread Pale Ale	= 11°
			Avg. Märzen/Oktoberfest	= 7 - 14°
	medium	10 - 14	Average Alt (Dusseldorf)	= 11 - 25°
	deep	14 - 20	Michelob Classic Dark	= 17°
Black		above 20	Salvator (Paulaner)	= 21°
			Triumphater (Lowenbrau)	= 29°
			Beliken Stout	= 76°

It is important to know that totally different units are used in England and Europe (i.e., degrees EBC). This is because of the different analytical procedures that are used for measurement. The following formulas have been used to relate these units:

$$(°EBC) = 2.65 \text{ x } (°L) - 1.2$$

$$(°L) = 0.377 \text{ x } (°EBC) + 0.45$$

I have found that they give reasonable results for light-colored beers (e.g., those whose color does not exceed 4 °L); however, they are inaccurate for deeper-colored beers. Discussions with Roger Briess of Briess Malting Company indicate that these formulas are not held in high regard by professionals.

INFLUENCE OF MALT

After the grain is steeped with water, it is allowed to germinate, then is dried in the kiln. It is in the kiln where coloring pigments such as melanoidins in malt are formed via the Maillard or browning reaction, a very common oxidation that occurs in many foods when they are cooked or exposed to air. By controlling the kiln temperature, the maltster can control the color of the kernels and hence their coloring potential in brewing. Typical values for various malt types are shown in Table 1.

A rule sometimes used by homebrewers is that the color contributed by a malt is equal to its concentration in pounds per gallon times its color rating in °L. For pale beers this rule can give reasonable results. For example, 10 pounds of pale malt with color 1.6 °L in five gallons should produce a beer whose color is near

$$1.6 \text{ x } 10/5 = 3.2°L.$$

But for darker colored beers this rule can give erratic results. It also ignores the factors other than malt that contribute to beer color. Cereal adjuncts like rice make no contribution to beer color. Corn and unmalted barley have only a slight effect.

TABLE 1. Typical °L values for different malt types.

Malt Type	Color °L
U.S. two-row	1.4 - 1.8
U.S. six-row	1.5 - 1.9
Canadian two-row	1.3 - 1.7
Canadian six-row	1.4 - 1.9
German Pils (two-row)	1.6
German lager (two-row)	1.7
CaraPils	1.3 - 1.8
Wheat malt	1.6 - 1.8
Pale ale	3
Vienna	3 - 5
Light Munich	8 - 11
Dark Munich	18 - 22
Caramel	10 - 120
Chocolate malt	325 - 375
Black	475 - 525
Black barley	500 - 550

INFLUENCE OF BREWING CONDITIONS

Differences in brewing conditions can lead to substantial color changes in the finished beer, these effects being particularly important for beers at 5 °L or less.

Water As the alkalinity of the water increases, so does the extraction rate of the coloring pigments in malt. The mash pH has the same effect, and increasing pH leads to worts with deeper color.

Mash Color increases with the amount of contact time with the grains. Thus, a prolonged mash will produce a deeper-colored beer than a short mash.

Kettle boil The Maillard reaction also takes place as wort is boiled; therefore, wort color increases with boil time. A fact that is sometimes overlooked is that wort simmering has the same effect. The point is that this will lead to an incomplete hot and cold break, which in turn leaves more coloring elements in the finished wort.

Hops Some color is obtained from hops both in the kettle and in storage containers when postfermentation hopping is used.

Fermentation The proteinous matter produced during the cold break is full of coloring materials and, hence, removal of these materials will reduce color. It has been reported that color changes during fermentation also vary with yeast strain.

Filtration This can dramatically reduce color. It should be noted that a clear beer will appear to be lighter in color than turbid beer.

Oxidation At all stages of brewing, air pickup will deepen beer color. This is as true of hot wort production as it is of bottled beer with head-space air.

BRIESS COLOR TEST

This is a simple test designed for homebrewers and microbrewers. Comparisons have shown that it will give color readings with errors more than one percent for beer whose color is 17 °L or less. Beers whose color exceeds 17 °L will be essentially black in appearance. It is not particularly important to quantify color beyond this point.

The standard for this test is Michelob Classic Dark. The reason is that it is widely available, and its color is known (17 °L). On very rare occasions one will come across old bottles of this beer where a haze has developed because of mishandling by distributors. These should not be used in this test. By the same token, the sample to be tested should be clear and free of haze.

The test consists of diluting the standard with water until a color match with the sample is obtained. Figure 2 gives the relationship between the amount of water added and the °L of the sample.

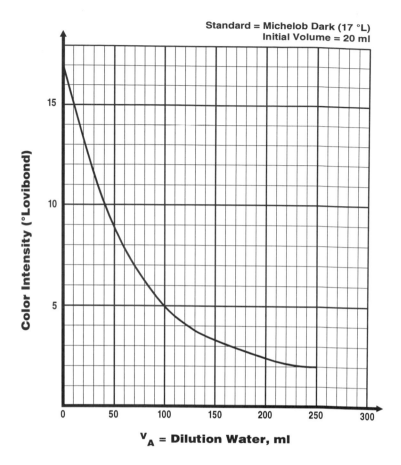

Standard = Michelob Dark (17 °L)
Initial Volume = 20 ml

Color Intensity (°Lovibond)

V_A = Dilution Water, ml

FIGURE 2. Amount of Water Added vs. °L

MATERIALS NEEDED

1. Distilled water — Colored tap water can increase the errors in this test from 1 percent to 10 or 20 percent.

2. Blender — Dissolved CO_2 in the beer will affect its color. Both the standard and the sample should be degassed. This can be done in a blender. A lot of foam will be created, but once it recedes and the beer falls clear it is ready for testing.

3. Light source — It is important for the visual comparison to take place in a well-lighted environment. Ideally, this consists of a lamp with a 100-watt bulb against a white background. Be sure to use the reflected rather than direct light, and place the samples the same distance from the light source. Also, take time in making the comparison because the difference in one or two °L is not that great.

4. Vessels — These are the most important components to this test. After extensive experimentation it became clear that two sets are needed. For detailed testing, two glass jars of one-inch diameter and a capacity of at least 125 milliliters are best. For samples below 10 °L the volume of these vessels is not large enough. Two white 12-ounce export (long neck) returnable bottles will be needed. The Miller Brewing Co. has been using these bottles. So has Corona, but the label, which cannot be removed, is a distraction.

5. Syringe — This is needed to measure 10 cc = 10 ml of water.

PROCEDURE

1. Clean everything.

2. De-gas standard and then sample in blender.

3. Measure in 20 ml of standard beer in export bottle No. 1.

4. Measure in 20 ml of sample beer in export bottle No. 2.

5. If colors are different, measure in 10 ml of distilled water to bottle No. 1 and 10 ml of sample beer to export bottle No. 2.

6. Continue Step 5 until colors become close. At this point the comparisons should be made in the one-inch diameter jars. Transfer 25 to 50 ml into these from the export bottles and return after comparison. Cut the water and sample beer increment from 10 ml to 5 ml.

7. When a color match is obtained, record the total amount of water added. Figure 2 gives the associated °L.

EXAMPLE – BASS PALE ALE

At the start the 20 ml of standard beer (Michelob Classic Dark) will be discernibly darker than the sample (Bass). After adding 30 ml of water to the standard, the colors will become close, and at this point the one-inch jars are needed. A match is obtained after an additional 10 ml of water is added. Thus a total of 40 ml of water was needed, and from Figure 2, we see that Bass has a color of 10 °L. Since only 60 ml of liquid was used in each bottle, the entire test could have done in the one-inch diameter jars.

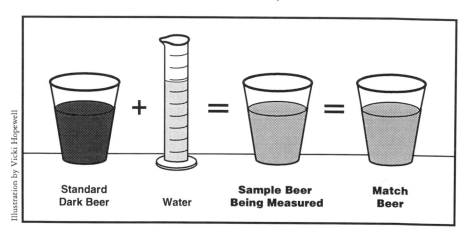

Standard Dark Beer   Water   Sample Beer Being Measured   Match Beer

Note that the relationship between °L and dilution water is not linear. For example, adding 20 ml of water to 20 ml of Michelob Classic Dark (17 °L) will not cut the color in half. In fact, instead of 17/2 = 8.5 °L the color will be higher, namely 13 °L (see Figure 2). This lack of proportionality is why the relationship between °L and degrees EBC can be in error. It also explains why beer color and malt color are not proportional.

At the lower color range, on the other hand, proportionality is approximately valid. Thus, diluting 20 ml of Molson Export Ale (4 °L) with 20 ml of water will give a color very close to Budweiser (2 °L). More generally for beers whose color is 4 °L or less, the curve in Figure 2 is given by

$$°L = 4(140/V_A + 20)$$

where V_A is the dilution water in ml.

(The author acknowledges the significant contributions made through conversations with Roger Briess. In fact, the simple color test described above is essentially his idea. The author's contribution was to work out the data represented in Figure 2.)

THE LANGUAGE OF
FLAVOR COMMUNICATION

CHARLIE PAPAZIAN

What is the purpose of communicating your knowledgeable opinions to the brewer when you're evaluating his or her beer in competitions or on flavor panels? The purposes of different tasting situations vary. As homebrewers, we're in a unique situation in that we brew and evaluate so many different styles of beer. We've taken a very big bite in the world of brewing when we brew a pale ale in the morning and a stout in the afternoon. That's a unique situation in the brewing community.

I brewed a Blitzweizen barley wine lager. What do you do with a beer like that? A weizen beer is not usually associated with a barley wine-style ale. Barley wine lager may never have existed before. But what I did when I brewed that beer was to have fun and to toy with the concept of styles.

What is the purpose of holding competitions? Certainly, one obvious purpose is to declare the winners — first, second, third, best-of-show, etc. But what do the winners represent? Whether or not a beer is judged the best stout in the category, or even the best-of-show, is nevertheless a subjective judgment. I think the winners represent the pride we homebrewers all have in what we're doing with our brewing, how we're talking about beer, and how we're enjoying introducing it to other people. I think that when we declare the winner, it's a representation of our appreciation of beer.

Another purpose, which is very important, is to inform the entrant about how his or her product stands out in your mind in comparison to the others you're judging. We can also give him our knowledgeable opinion on how he can improve his or her beer.

If it's a look-alike competition that we're judging, we can tell entrants how close or far off the mark they are in reproducing the target product. For example, this year's competition featured a Chimay Belgian look-alike category. These are beers that are trying to taste, look, sound and feel like a Chimay.

The third interesting aspect of competition is gaining useful data. Through holding the National Competition, we have compiled an enormous amount of information including recipes, the brewing equipment used by entrants, ingredients, and what types of homebrewers are winning competitions, to name a few.

GOING BY THE SCORE SHEET

To communicate to a person entered in a competition, we use a score sheet. And the precursor to being able to use that tool is knowing four things. The first is having knowledge of beer styles. In my opinion, this is the foremost prerequisite. I don't see how anyone can judge in a homebrewed beer competition without knowing the history and parameters of styles.

Another requisite, which is quite obvious, is having a trained palate. You should be able to detect various aromatic and flavor components, to recognize the appropriate appearance of a beer, and to determine whether it is on the mark for that category. In a sense, the eyes are a palate and the ears are a palate. Those of you who might be new to brewing may not think that this makes sense. But those of us who have experienced a number of different beers know that it's okay to have a chill haze in some styles of beers.

Third, to effectively judge homebrewed beer, knowledge of the brewing process is paramount in being able to evaluate the beer and inform the brewer about what he or she might do to change the product in the way in which you, as the judge, would advise. That's your position in a homebrew competition. People on flavor panels in various food industries — beer, wine, mustard, dairy products — may not need to know the process. But we have that responsibility. Likewise, the beer judge must also know the ingredients of beer.

COMMUNICATION - ANOTHER ELEMENT

So you take all those elements of responsibility and then you top them off with this fifth component — communication. You need to be able to gather all the information listed above and then integrate it so you can communicate its most important aspects to the brewer. This is perhaps the most difficult task of beer evaluators.

You can go to a class and train yourself to taste salt, butter, sour, grassy, musty, etc. That's straightforward. But to also have the historical sense of what the beer should be like — and also have the knowledge of where the good or bad flavors come from — makes you a very valuable evaluator. It's a challenge. For years, people have been pushing beers in front of me asking for my opinion. They may have a raspberry-flavored stout, a rootbeer-flavored pale ale, and then a garlic-flavored old ale. I can't help but think that must be very intimidating for a first-time judge. It's intimidating to have that amount of responsibility.

One person on our staff just began judging and was faced with the task of judging American Pilseners and European light lagers. One day she was quietly sitting at the table toiling over some paperwork when she said, "Must I be trying to smell diacetyl in my coffee?"

When you get involved, what you're experiencing transcends into other areas of your life. You have these four elements — style, knowledge, palate training, brewing process, and ingredients used — which you are trying to integrate.

How should you feel when you're judging and writing your comments on a score sheet. Are you totally removed from the identity of the person who brewed the beer? I wondered to myself the other day, if Michael Jackson were to take up homebrewing and you knew that you were going to judge his first homebrew, going to give him a score, going to put comments on his score sheet, would you feel any differently about evaluating his beer than about evaluating an anonymous beer? No matter whose beer it is, we should be as responsible and careful as possible.

EXAMPLES IN EVALUATION

I'm going to isolate the various components of evaluation and go over the process of scoring a beer with respect to style and history, the brewing process, the ingredients — all the aspects you must take into perspective when you evaluate a beer. I'll use our American Homebrewers Association Beer Score Sheet, (see page 54) but I won't be taking into consideration any of the number scoring.

Let's take British bitter, for example, and look at it in respect to the score sheet. Think about what we'd consider in evaluating appearance, bouquet, and flavor, leaving out the process and ingredients for now.

What should it be as far as clarity? It can have a slight chill haze. It shouldn't be cooled below 55 degrees F (15.5 degrees C), and if you know the style, you know that a chill haze is acceptable. Color? A British bitter can range from a pale ale to almost dark amber. Also traditionally, bitters do not have a lot of carbonation and therefore not much foam. It doesn't necessarily have a flat head, either. There are styles of bitter in England that have as much as half an inch of head on top that looks very creamy. There are also bitters in the south of Britain that have no head; the glass is filled right to the rim. Knowing the style, I can't knock the beer I'm judging unless it is completely flat or all foam. A little foam or no foam is acceptable.

What should the bouquet/aroma of a bitter be? Some have a very hoppy aroma, others have no hop aroma. You have to know the style.

As far as flavor and hop/malt balance, I've visited England twice and after drinking British bitter I could smack my lips and still taste the bitterness. That's one way I judge bitterness. It should have a full shot of bitterness. It shouldn't be too mild.

In judging body, British bitter shouldn't be too sweet. If you get a very sweet, full-bodied beer in the bitter category, maybe you should recommend that it be entered in another category. You need knowledge of the style so that when you score low or make a comment that may not be favorable, you can back up your comments with knowledge.

As for other fermentation characteristics, British bitter is an ale. Simplistically, ales are top-fermenting and have a fruitiness. Therefore, British bitter should have a degree of fruitiness. There are hundreds of types of bitters and you need to recognize that and not play favorites with your own palate. Use what has been written as your standard.

Aftertaste? As I mentioned, there's that bitter flavor on your lips.

Now let's run through the judging categories with regards to bock beers. As for clarity, bock is a lager, it is cold-fermented and should therefore be clear. Stylistically, bock shouldn't have a chill haze. Bock can also be very pale or chocolaty-brown. There's that whole range of color to consider in your comments. Bock is a German beer, and as such, should have a reasonable head.

Bouquet/aroma? Bock has more of a malty nose to it than a hoppiness. The malt should predominate. The body should be full and should stylistically reflect more alcohol. If you've practiced, you can detect the presence of alcohol in the aroma, and if it is a correct bock beer, you'll notice the alcohol smell.

A bock beer shouldn't have alelike characteristics. Often homebrewers don't have the ability to cold ferment, so they ferment at high temperatures with a lager yeast. Or maybe they use ale yeast, or whatever they can get. If you can detect it, you can say, "This smells like banana. It might be good for another style of beer, but not for bock." That's your responsibility as a judge.

Let's look at the process in regards to two beers. First, American Pilsener. What can be done in the brewing process to make American Pilsener as clear as it should be? Some homebrewers filter it to get rid of the chill haze or yeast. You can also cold lager it to precipitate the chill haze before you bottle it.

In regard to color, if it is too dark, you may communicate to the brewer that although he or she may have used the lightest malt, maybe the wort was boiled too long and caramelized until it became amber colored. Or maybe the brewer used too much black malt.

What about the bouquet? When considering the process of brewing American Pilseners, if you detect fermentation characteristics that are too strongly estery, you could suggest cooler fermentation temperatures or aeration of the wort.

Look at the hop/malt balance and the body. If you're tasting an American Pilsener that is very sweet and full-bodied, you know that stylistically it's improper. How did the characteristic get into the beer and how could the beer be made better? Mashing at higher temperatures gives a fuller-bodied beer. You might want to suggest along these lines. Or maybe the brewer used too much malt extract or used a brand having too many dextrins.

Let's take strong ales for an example with regard to process. I don't want to touch on clarity with a strong beer except that stylistically, Belgian strong beers may be hazy because they are bottle conditioned. That's acceptable.

One thing you should find in the bouquet/aroma of a strong ale is a high percentage of alcohol. You should be able to smell it. If you don't,

you should tell the brewer how to pull that into his or her product. Perhaps the brewer didn't aerate the wort enough and starved the yeast, causing sluggish fermentation. Suggest that he or she aerate the wort.

Hop/malt balance and body? Strong ales can have varying degrees of full body. You have beers like Duvel, which is a medium-bodied beer, and then you have barley wine ales, which are very full-bodied. What can you suggest to the brewer? Mashing temperatures contribute to the final fullness of the beer.

If you have a strong ale in which you can detect no real estery characteristics, no alelike characteristics, then maybe it was fermented very cold like a lager and it doesn't belong in the strong ale category. Fermentation for strong ales should ideally be in the 55 to 65 degrees F (13 to 18.5 degrees C) range in order to get the alelike characteristics.

Moving on to ingredients, let's take Oktoberfest, for example. An Oktoberfest should be clear and the ingredients should be all barley malt. If there's a chill haze, maybe the brewer used some wheat. If an Oktoberfest is too pale, you might suggest using more toasted malt. If it is as dark as brown ale or stout, maybe you could suggest cutting back on malt.

How can the ingredients affect the bouquet/aroma of an Oktoberfest? It should have a malt aroma. If not, suggest that the brewer add freshly toasted, malted barley to the mash or brewing process.

In regard to the hop/malt balance, if you know the style, you know that Munich or toasted malts should be used. These affect the taste, which should be malty but slightly bitter.

These are the considerations that go through my mind when I try to communicate what I'm evaluating to the brewer whose beer I'm judging.

You need to clearly define what it is you want to communicate. I believe that we all have the responsibility to help the brewer learn more about his or her product. Judging homebrew is complicated and takes practice and training to accomplish. I've never stopped learning about beer evaluation.

WHAT TO AIM FOR
IN FLAVOR PROFILING

CHARLIE PAPAZIAN

"I like it." "I don't like it." "I want a *good* beer." "This beer is bad." Gone are the days when phrases such as these served to communicate the taste of beer among homebrewers. Now we know too much.

We discuss ingredients, processes, equipment, handling, tastes, aroma, appearance and so many other elements, all serving to provide a kind of résumé of the beers we make and the beers we drink. You'd think that maybe, with all of this knowledge, our avocation would get out of hand. This doesn't seem to be the case.

We've come so far that now we are able to communicate among ourselves as American homebrewers over an area of 3.6 million square miles. That is quite phenomenal when you think about it. An amateur brewer in Maine communicating with homebrewers in South Dakota, Southern California and Louisiana so definitively that a specific brew could conceivably be made in all four areas — by amateurs! All for the love of beer.

The information we are communicating about the flavor of beer can be neatly organized for special purposes. Brewers, both professional and amateurs, have been doing it for years, each for their own very special reasons. This organization of thoughts and perception is called "flavor profiling."

A flavor profile is a snapshot of our sensory experience, or what we anticipate to be our sensory experience. It is the sum of many parts. It is not a linear measurement of high or low, yes or no, dark or light, detectable or not detectable, balanced or not balanced. It is not a number nor is it a score. It is an attempt to define the soul of a beer. It is the sum of many things, both desirable and undesirable, it is an expression of reasoning and the unknown, and here we are, the homebrewer, the beer lover, trying to communicate how and why beer is what it is. As beer lovers and brewers, we peculiarly enjoy the discourse of talking to each other, especially in an uncoded, clear fashion.

BEER CHARACTERISTICS

Sweet
low ☐☐☐☐☐☐ high
Bitter
low ☐☐☐☐☐☐ high
Alcohol
low ☐☐☐☐☐☐ high
Body
light ☐☐☐☐☐☐ full
Fruity-estery
low ☐☐☐☐☐☐ high
Diacetyl
low ☐☐☐☐☐☐ high
Sour-acidic
low ☐☐☐☐☐☐ high
DMS
low ☐☐☐☐☐☐ high
Color
light ☐☐☐☐☐☐ dark

Illustration by Vicki Hopewell

The state-of-the-art leads me to believe there are two primary reasons today's homebrewers are interested in describing the character of beer: first, flavor profiling can be used to define a style; second, flavor profiling can be used to describe any one beer and to communicate what it is we are tasting and how it got there.

In a perfect world it would be nice to learn about the characters of a certain type of beer, brew it and enjoy it exactly as it was intended to be. Flavor profiles can be helpful guideposts in this way. Unfortunately (or perhaps more appropriately — fortunately) we live in a real world with real ale and real beer, and beer does not always turn out exactly as we intended it to. An analysis of the flavor of our beers based on what is perceived by our senses is the most useful type of flavor profile for those who wish to learn more about their beer.

Before a flavor profile can be useful we must all agree on language.

In recent years homebrewers and beer lovers have developed a tremendous interest in the world's beer styles so a vocabulary has been developed to better describe the taste of these styles. We've begun to profile the flavor characteristics of the world's beer styles.

In writing a dictionary of beer styles we might look at nine or ten very measurable flavor characters and develop a useful flavor profile for any beer style in the world. It is helpful to use the same system for all of the beers that are to be compared. With the help of avid homebrewer and friend, Glenn Hamburg, I have developed a list of nine (plus one special category) definably singular sensory descriptors that I believe can be used to help profile the world's classic beer styles. (See Table 1.)

By rating each of the Beer Flavor Style Profile descriptors from 1 (low) to 10 (high), one can quite accurately profile most beer styles. Of course, many more could be added to this list, but I have found that adding such secondary descriptors as carbonation level, hop aroma or clarity usually serve to more specifically define subcategories or describe recognized or allowable variations in a main style. The special descriptor may be used to specify such character as "smoky" in a German Rauchbier or "cherries" in a Belgian kriek.

The combination of the 10 categories are endless, and I don't believe there are any two styles of beer that would have the identical profile, using a system such as this.

Let's try profiling Barley Wine Ales and American Pilseners, two quite different styles. (See Table 1.)

TABLE 1. Sensory Descriptors

ON A SCALE OF 1 TO 10

Sweet	low	— high	
Bitter	low	— high	
Alcohol	low	— high	
Body	light	— full	
Fruity-Estery	low	— high	(flavor and aroma)
Diacetyl	low	— high	
Sour-Acidic	low	— high	
DMS	low	— high	
Color	light	— dark	(not actually flavor but included here for defining styles)
Special descriptor	low	— high	

BARLEY WINE ALE

Sweet	low	— high	7-10 rating (high)
Bitter	low	— high	5-10 rating (medium to high)
Alcohol	low	— high	8-10 rating (high)
Body	light	— full	7-10 rating (full)
Fruity-Estery	low	— high	7-10 rating (high)
Diacetyl	low	— high	1-2 rating (low)
Sour-Acidic	low	— high	0 rating (none)
DMS	low	— high	0 rating (none)
Color	light	— dark	3-6 rating (amber to brown)
Special descriptor		none	

AMERICAN PILSENER

Sweet	low	— high	1-3 rating (low)
Bitter	low	— high	2-3 rating (low)
Alcohol	low	— high	2-3 rating (low)
Body	light	— full	1-3 rating (light)
Fruity-Estery	low	— high	1-2 rating (low)
Diacetyl	low	— high	0 rating (none)
Sour-Acidic	low	— high	0 rating (none)
DMS	low	— high	1 rating (very low)
Color	light	— dark	1-2 rating (light)
Special descriptor		none	

As mentioned earlier, the real world is not so kind. Because more than 400 recognizable flavors have been isolated in beer, and because the brewing process can be so variably unkind, we often find ourselves with curious beer flavors and many questions.

When profiling our own beer, as amateur brewers, the Beer Flavor Style Profile often is not adequate. A list of descriptors can be developed to measure the characters of beer most important to the homebrewer. The purpose is to be most helpful to the homebrewer in understanding the factors influencing the production of beer flavors.

Beware — a competition score sheet measures how accurately your beer has been made and expresses that in a linear numerical way. Scoring beer in a competition format is not an appropriate means of expressing flavor profile. The beer flavor descriptor definitions on page 12 could be helpful for profiling most homebrewed beer in America.

A beer flavor profile should clearly show how a beer tastes. We can take a beer flavor profile one more step and make it even more useful to the brewer by relating the flavor components to their possible origins in the ingredients, process, equipment, handling and packaging of the beer.

Accompanying this article is a troubleshooter's chart that briefly outline how ingredients, process, equipment, handling and packaging may influence the beer's flavor profile. But brewers should beware — solutions to problems are many and arguable, even among the professionals whom we like to call "experts." But even they realize there are no experts when it comes to defining flavor and their origins. These descriptors and charts are meant to be helpful guides and not necessarily "the" solution to your problems.

Troubleshooter's Chart

A BREWERS GUIDE TO BETTER BEER

This chart is intended for use by brewers as a guide in helping to identify the causes of certain more commonly occurring beer flavors. It is not intended to represent a complete compilation of beer flavors or their origins. Published by the American Homebrewers Association.

Profile Descriptor	Ingredients	Process	Equipment	Handling and processing
Alcohol (ethanol) — *a warming prickly sensation in the mouth and throat.*	High: increase fermentable sugars through use of malt or adjuncts. NOTE: use of corn, rice, sugar, honey adds alcohol without adding body. High: healthy and attenuative yeast strains.	High: within the general 145 to 158 degree F range of mashing temperatures the lower mash temperature produce more fermentables, thus more resulting alcohol. High: aeration of wort before pitching aids yeast activity. High: fusel (solventlike) alcohols are produced at high temperatures.		Age and oxidation will convert some of the ethanol to higher solventlike alcohols.
Astringent — *(see Husky/Grainy)*				
Bitter — *a sensation generally perceived on the back of the tongue, and sometimes roof of the mouth, as with caffeine or hop resin.*	High: black and roasted malts and grains. High: great amounts of boiling hops. High: alkaline water can draw out bitter components from grains.	High: effective boiling of hops. Low: high fermentation temperatures and quick fermentation rates will decrease hop bitterness.	Low: filtration can remove some bitterness.	

Profile Descriptor	Ingredients	Process	Equipment	Handling and processing
Body — *not a flavor but a sensation of viscosity in the mouth as with thick (full-bodied) beers or thin (light-bodied) beers.*	**Full:** use of malto-dextrin, dextrinous malts, lactose, crystal malt, caramel malt, dextrine (CaraPils) malt. **Thin:** use of highly fermentable malt. **Thin:** use of enzymes that break down carbohydrates in mash, fermentation or storage.	**Full:** high-temperature mash. **Low:** low-temperature mash.		**Low:** age will reduce body. **Low:** wild yeast and bacteria may reduce body by breaking down carbohydrates.
Clarity — *visual perception of the beer in the bottle and after it is poured.*	**High:** use of protein reducing enzymes (papain). **Low:** chill haze more likely in all-malt beers because higher protein than malt and adjunct beers. **Low:** wheat malt and unmalted barley cause more chill haze than malted barley and corn and rice adjuncts. **Low:** poor flocculant wild yeast may cause poor sedimentation. **Low:** bacteria causes cloudiness and haze. **High:** use of polyclar or activated silica gel.	**Low:** overmilling/grinding grain. **High:** long, vigorous boil and proper cooling.	**Low:** bacteria from dirty plastic equipment, especially siphon and blow-out hoses, scratched fermenter. **High:** filtration can help clear.	**Low:** unclean bottles can cause bacterial haze.
Color — *visual perception of beer color.*	**Dark:** dark malts (crystal, Munich, chocolate, roasted barley, black patent). **Light:** exclusive use of lighter malts and starch adjuncts.	**Dark:** scorching. **Dark:** caramelization with long boil.	**Low:** filtration can reduce color.	

Profile Descriptor	Ingredients	Process	Equipment	Handling and processing
Degree of Carbonation	High: bacteria and wild yeast may break down carbohydrates not normally fermentable and create overcarbonation and gushing. High: over priming. NOTE ON GUSHING: excessive iron content causes gushing; malts containing Fusarium (mold) from wet harvesting of barley causes gushing; precipitates of excess salts in bottle cause gushing.	Low: cold temperatures inhibit ale yeast. Low: long lagered beer may not have enough viable yeast for bottle conditioning (carbonating) properly.	High: unsanitary equipment can introduce bacteria which can cause overcarbonation and gushing.	High: unclean bottles can cause bacterial growth and gushing. High: overpriming kegs; prime kegs at one third normal rate. High: agitation. Low: improper seal on bottle cap.
Diacetyl — *butter or butterscotch flavor.*	High: unhealthy, non-flocculating yeast. High: not enough soluble nitrogen-based yeast nutrient in wort. High: not enough oxygen in wort when pitching yeast. High: bacterial contamination. High/Low: yeast strain will influence production of diacetyl. High: excessive use of adjuncts such as corn or rice, deficient in amino acid (soluble nitrogen-based nutrients).	High: chilling fermentation too soon. High: high-temperature initial fermentation. High: premature fining takes yeast out of suspension too soon. Low: agitated extended fermentation. Low: high temperature during extended fermentation. Low: kraeusening.	High: bacteria from equipment. High/Low: configuration and size of fermenting vessel will influence production.	

Profile Descriptor	Ingredients	Process	Equipment	Handling and processing
Dimethylsulfide (DMS) — *cooked cabbage or sweet cornlike.*	**High:** high-moisture malt, especially six-row varieties. **High:** bacterial contamination of wort. **Low:** use a two-row English malt. **High:** under pitching of yeast (lag time). **High:** bacterially infected yeast slurry.	**Low:** longer boil will diminish DMS. **High:** oversparging at low temperatures (especially lower than 160 degrees F or 71 degrees C).	**High:** bacteria from equipment.	**High:** introduction of unfiltered CO_2 produced by fermentation. Bottle priming will produce small amounts.
Fruity/Estery — *flavors similar to fruits such as: strawberry, banana, raspberry, apple, pear.*	Yeast strains produce various esters. **High:** loaded with fruit.	**High:** excessive trub. **High:** warm fermentation. **High:** high pitching rates. **High:** high-gravity wort. **High:** excessive aeration of wort. **Low:** opposite of above.		**Low:** age will reduce esters to closely related fusel alcohols and acids (solventlike qualities).
Head Retention — *physical and visual degree of foam stability.*	**Good:** high malt content. **Poor:** use of overmodified or underkilned malt. **Good:** mashing in of barley flakes. **Good:** licorice, crystal malt, dextrine (CaraPils) malt, wheat malt. **Good:** high bittering hops in boil. **Poor:** hard water. **Poor:** germ oil in whole grain. **Poor:** elevated volumes of higher alcohols. **Good:** high nitrogen content.	**Low:** oversparging (releases fatty acids). **Low:** excessive aeration of wort before pitching. **Low:** extended enzymic molecular breakdown of carbohydrates in mashing. **Low:** fatty acid release during yeast autolysis. **Low:** high fermentation temperatures (production of higher alcohols). **High:** good rolling boil in kettle.	**Poor:** cleaning residues, improper rinsing of fats, oils, detergents, soaps. **Poor:** filtration can reduce head retention.	**Low:** oxidation/aging breaks down head stabilizing agents. **Low:** dirty bottles, improperly rinsed. **Low:** improperly cleaned glasses.

Profile Descriptor	Ingredients	Process	Equipment	Handling and processing
Husky/Grainy (Astringent bitter) — *raw grainlike flavor, dry, puckerlike sensation as in grape tannin.*	**High:** alkaline or high sulfate water. **High:** stems and skins of fruit. **High:** six-row more than two-row malt.	**High:** oversparging grains. **High:** boiling grains. **High:** excess trub. **High:** poor hot brew (improper boiling). **High:** overmilling/grinding. **High:** high temperature (above 175 degrees F or 79.5 degrees C) sparge water.		**Low:** aging reduces astringency.
Light struck (skunky) — *like a skunk (the British describe this character as "catty" because there are no skunks in the U.K.).*	**High:** some varieties of hops.		**High:** fermenting beer in glass carboy in bright light.	**High:** light striking beer through green or clear glass and over a prolonged time through brown glass. NOTE: effect is instantaneous with clear or green glass.
Metallic — *tinny, coinlike, bloodlike.*	**High:** iron content in water.		**High:** mild steel, aluminum, cast iron. **High:** cleaning stainless steel or copper without subsequently oxidizing surfaces to form a protective layer of oxide on metal.	
Oxidation — *paper or cardboardlike, winy, sherrylike, rotten pineapple or rotten vegetables.*	**Low:** addition of ascorbic acid (Vitamin C).	**High:** aeration when siphoning or pumping. **High:** adding tap or aerated water to finished beer.	**High:** malfunctioning airlock.	**High:** too much air space in bottle. **High:** warm temperatures. **High:** age.
Phenolic — *medicinal, bandaidlike, smokey, clovelike, plasticlike.*	**High:** chlorinated (tap) water. **High:** wild yeast. **High:** bacteria. **High:** wheat malt (clovelike) or roasted barley/malts (smoky).	**High:** oversparging of mash. **High:** boiling grains.	**High:** cleaning compound residue. **High:** plastic hoses and gaskets. **High:** bacterial and wild yeast contamination.	**High:** defective bottlecap linings.

Profile Descriptor	Ingredients	Process	Equipment	Handling and processing
Salty — *sensation generally perceived on the sides of the tongue as with table salt (sodium chloride).*	**High:** brewing salts, particularly those containing sodium chloride (table salt) and magnesium sulfate (epsom salts).			
Sour/Acidic — *sensation generally perceived on the sides of the tongue as with lemon juice (citric acid).*	**High:** introduction of lactobacillus, acetobacter and other acid-forming bacteria. **High:** too much refined sugar. **High:** addition of citric acid. **High:** excessive ascorbic acid (Vitamin C).	**High:** mashing too long promotes bacterial growth and acid byproducts in mash. **High:** bacteria in wort, fermentation. **High:** excessive fermentation temperatures promotes bacterial growth. **Low:** sanitize all equipment.	**High:** bacteria harbored in scratched surfaces of plastic, glass, stainless, improper welds, valves, spigots, gaskets, discolored plastic. **High:** use of wooden spoon in cooled wort or fermentation.	**High:** storage at warm temperatures. **High:** unsanitary bottles or kegs.
Sulfur — *sulfur dioxide, hydrogen sulfide (rotten eggs), see DMS, see skunk, yeastlike flavor.*	**High:** various yeast strains will produce byproducts. **High:** malt releases minor amounts.	**High:** yeast autolysis; sedimented yeast in contact with beer in fermenter too long. **High/Low:** yeast strains will influence.		
Sweet — *sensation generally perceived on the tip of the tongue as with sucrose (white table sugar).*	**High:** high malt content. **High:** crystal malt, Munich malt and toasted malt create sweet malt flavor. **High:** low hopping. **High:** licorice. **High:** low attenuation or unhealthy yeast strains.	**High:** within the general 145- to 150-degree-F (63- to 65.5-degree-C) range of mashing temperatures the higher mash temperatures produce more unfermentable carbohydrates.		**Low:** aging reduces sweetness.

BEER EVALUATION TECHNIQUES:
GETTING THE MOST FROM YOUR BEER

GROSVENOR MERLE-SMITH

I will take you through the beer evaluation process as we homebrew judges do it. This will provide you with a procedure to follow every time you taste a beer, whether or not it is in a formal situation. What I do hope is that anytime you sit down and taste a beer, you will think about it with regard to those evaluation procedures.

First of all, when you sit down to a beer, you want to know what type it is stylistically. Hopefully, you have in your mind the parameters of the style because you will be tasting the beer in relation to what you already know.

You need to have a good idea of what the brewing procedures are for each style of beer. You need to know the use of all the individual ingredients and how they affect the beer. With this knowledge, you can decipher the characteristics of the beer to further evaluate it.

To be at your best, you must be well-rested, particularly if you will be evaluating beer in a formal tasting. Fatigue makes your assessment of beer much more difficult. When you sit down to judge, you need to pace yourself, and if you quickly go through a dozen beers, you should maintain a sense of freshness throughout.

You should come into a tasting with a clean mouth. A number of factors destroy both your ability to taste and many aspects of your beer. Bacteria in your mouth (living on food particles lodged in your teeth) create a highly acidic condition, which will taint your tasting. Greasy food, oil or lipstick coat your mouth and dull your sense of perception, and they also devastate the head-retention qualities of your beer. For example, if you stick your nose in the foam, it will create a crater and destroy the head on the beer. Approach the job of judging beer by being well groomed.

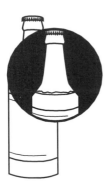

The room in which the judging will take place should be quiet, cool and well-lit. White table-cloths give a good contrast to beer color, and candles can be used for extra light. There should be no evidence of odors or smoke in the room, and you should refrain from wearing perfume or scented soap. The purpose of these instructions is to give yourself a good, clean foundation so you can perceive the qualities of the beer.

Most of the literature prescribes using a good, beer-clean glass. An alternative is to use a high-grade, clear, hard-plastic cup. As much as anyone disparages the idea of using plastic, it is consistent and fairly free of any alien odors. If there is any residual plastic aroma, at least it is consistent throughout the judging.

Before you settle down to judge, be sure you have writing utensils, score sheets, openers and bread to cleanse your palate. Dump buckets are a necessary receptacle for dumping beer and containing foaming beer.

Essentially the score sheet is used to guide you through an evaluation of a beer using all your senses. (See pages 53 and 54 for sample score sheet.) In AHA competitions, the bottles are available to the

Illustration by Vicki Hopewell

judges because we believe that you can learn a lot from opening the beer, seeing it in the bottle, and pouring it. You can tell if the cap is appropriately put on, and then when you pour the beer, you can hear how it sounds. The size of the bubbles also give a clue as to how the beer will taste.

In pouring beer into the glass, I like to flop a dollop of beer into the bottom of the glass and take a look at whether it is very carbonated. Once I have a sense of that, I tip the glass and pour the beer down the side so I don't get excessive head.

There are several opinions on the best way to pour beer: straight into the middle or dribbling it down the side. In my opinion, the best way is a combination of the two. An appropriate amount of head is necessary — half an inch to an inch and a half — to take some carbonation out of the beer and release the aromatic volatiles that are important to your initial impression of the beer.

After the beer has been poured, assess the aromatics. Put your nose in the glass and take a good sharp whiff, filling your sinuses. Don't keep sniffing, or your olfactory sense will very quickly become dull. If you need to smell it again after the initial whiff, take a few deep breaths of air, then sniff the beer once more.

In the aroma you want to try to confirm the perceptions you had in mind when you poured it and watched it foam up. If it was excessively carbonated, then perhaps you will smell an infection. Think about the ingredients of the beer. For instance, if you are judging a fruit beer, does the fruit essence come through? Malt? Hops? Is the aroma appropriate for the category? Remember that you are judging for the appropriateness of category and cleanliness of the technical brewing process. One thing we notice in the competition is that many of the beers could have been brewed cleaner than they were.

Having made that assessment, you have the time to go back and evaluate the appearance. Is the beer clear? Is the color appropriate? How is the head: is it maintaining or dissipating? At this point, you should have a very, very good idea of the individual beer. In fact, I can just about complete the score sheet before I ever actually taste the beer. Then I taste the beer almost to confirm my analysis. In each step of the way, you make an assessment, and then see whether it leads to the next step in your assessment. Did it fool you? Or does the next step confirm your findings?

Take a fairly good sip of beer and move it around your mouth. You want the beer to contact all the parts of your mouth because your mouth perceives different qualities of flavor in different areas: sweet on the tip of the tongue; salt on the sides; astringent under the tongue; bitter on the back; etc. Pay attention to each of these areas to evaluate the flavor you are tasting. Beer is so complex that you must consciously dwell on each of these possibilities to see if they are present. Is the mouthfeel appropriate to the style? Are the ingredients you taste appropriate? Once you have perceived these flavors, swallow the beer, then think about any lingering aftertastes.

The last thing is, think about your overall impression of the beer. Would you like to continue drinking it? Once, when I was in Mexico, I ran across two fellows sitting in a restaurant drinking bottle after bottle of Pacifico. They were fairly inebriated, and I struck up a conversation and found out they had been there for three days testing the drinkability of Pacifico. They did decide, in fact, that they would serve Pacifico in the restaurant.

QUALITY AND TYPE OF COMMENTS

You should be able to go back, review the score sheets you have completed, and be able to say, "I remember that beer." This should be the case whether you are judging in a competition, or evaluating beer for your own education. In essence, you should create your experience of that beer on the score sheet.

For example, if a score sheet that rates a beer excellent, with a score of 45, and the only comment is, "You're doing everything right. Keep it up," you wouldn't be able to identify which beer it was for. On another score sheet, the comment is, "Cut down on the dark grains." Neither of these say much of anything to the brewer.

A third one says, "It's amazing how clear this beer is. You'd impress any brewmaster." It goes on to say, "This is best-of-show quality. Clean aroma, nice lager characters, nice dense head, excellent, excellent balance. Don't change anything, but if you did, maybe 10 percent more hops would be nice." This doesn't say much about the beer, but it does list the judge's perception of the beer. If you were receiving this evaluation of your beer, you would be a lot more tickled to get this one than either of the first two.

Another says, "Very estery. This is a warm ferment. Has a nice fruity character almost like some Trappist ales. Attractive color, and nice, creamy, small-bubbled head."

A fifth says, "Wow! Heavy hops. This brew has too much residual bitterness. Cut way back on the boiling hops. If you really like hops, use more for finishing. This will reduce the bitterness and hike up the bouquet in the floral, hop-flavored characters. Hops boiled for more than about five minutes rapidly lose those nifty volatiles that I guess you love. Other than that, it's a pretty tasty brew. Try it again."

You still don't have a sense of what that beer was from reading this score sheet, but you have a good understanding of the judge's feelings and why. The important thing here is "why?"

How do judges handle evaluating a bad beer? Here is a score sheet that says, "Too many harsh flavors. Yeasty, sour. Very red color, not dark enough." The final score was less than 20, which is considered a problem beer.

Another one says, "The clarity is good. Beer has nice fruity, estery qualities. Spiky, banana, clovelike aroma due to warm temperatures for wild yeast or possible contamination. Also solventlike aroma from warm ferment. Too dark for category. Use lighter malts. Possibly uses sugar; avoid if so. Contaminated. Pay more attention to sanitation. Problems are very definitive. Warm fermentation, sugar, contamination, some oxidation."

Here the judge has made an effort to communicate with the brewer. I don't believe that there was the same effort on the other examples. This judge is genuinely making a heartfelt effort to help the brewer, not putting him on the spot. This should be the feeling you try to convey through your score sheets.

It is important that you judge with humility and respect the brewer who made a great effort to send his or her beer into competition. Many brewers are just beginning to brew, and it may be difficult for them to get valuable information. This is your opportunity to give it to them. Assume that the brewer is doing his or her best. He or she would probably like to make better beer, but may not know how.

Finally, with regard to formal judging, it is extremely important that both the stewards and the judges make certain that the score sheets are completed. It is very important to keep your speed up when you are judging. Spend five minutes on a beer, for example, finish with it, and move on to the next one. You don't have the time in a formal competition to spend fifteen minutes mulling over each entry.

Try not to be too intimidated by the judging process. Beer is extremely complex, and judging beer is a life-long process. If you don't know the reason for a certain characteristic in a beer, don't worry about it; just see if you can find out later. It is important that you make the effort to find out. Learning about beer evaluation will teach you a better vocabulary, and will help you remember information about beer styles and flavor.

The Beer Judge Certification Program was established in 1985 to recognize homebrewers and beer lovers who have a thorough understanding of the brewing process, the flavor components of beer and the historical development of world beer styles. The BJCP has helped establish a universal language for judging beer as well as consistent procedures and scoring systems for all beer judgings across the country.

As of 1993, to participate in the BJCP, prospective judges must take a three-hour, two-part examination consisting of essay questions and a tasting. Judges may then gain experience points by judging in sanctioned competitions throughout the country and moving up through the ranks of the program.

For more information on the BJCP, contact the American Homebrewers Association, PO Box 1679, Boulder, CO 80306-1679 phone: (303) 447-0816, FAX: (303) 447-2825. The BJCP is co-sponsored by the American Homebrewers Association and the Home Wine and Beer Trade Association.

PERCEIVING FLAVOR:
TECHNIQUES FOR RECOGNIZING
BEER'S SUBTLE FLAVOR COMPONENTS

JIM KOCH

FLAVOR PROFILE OF BEER

To me, malt and hops are the heart and soul of beer flavor. Beer is fundamentally a combination of the sweetness and body of the malt — that is the heart, and the spiciness and bitterness of the hops — the soul. Of course, there are other major variables, such as the use of caramel or black malt, the fermentation temperatures, the type of hops used, the timing of adding the hops, and infinite minor variables. But to me, of first importance are the malt and the hops.

I believe malt and hops are so important that they shed light on beer styles in an objective way. But to do that, the malt and hop content must be measured in a quantifiable way. Hop content is fairly straightforward: it is normally measured in International Bitterness Units (IBU). One IBU is one part per million of isohumulones in the beer. IBUs actually measure something slightly different than simple bitterness. This is because really good hops produce isohumulones that don't taste so starkly bitter, while cheap hops produce very bitter isohumulones.

There are other components of hop flavor besides simple bitterness. Hops added early in the boil produce more bitter taste at the same IBU level than hops added later. And I think the same thing is true of hop extract: it tastes more bitter at the same IBU level.

Malt content can be measured in several ways such as original gravity, real extract, and apparent extract. I believe that what you really taste and feel in your mouth is best measured as apparent extract. The malt content in finished beer can be measured with a saccharometer. The saccharometer reading in finished beer is the apparent extract.

Actually, a saccharometer is a very useful tool. Most homebrewers don't utilize its potential, but remember that it is just about the only tool all brewers had for many years. For example, the saccharometer is all that is needed to measure alcohol, real extract and calories in beer. Take the original gravity and subtract the apparent extract. Then multiply that figure by 0.43, which will give the approximate alcohol by weight of the beer:

Original Gravity - Apparent Extract x 0.43 = Alcohol by Weight

For example: OG - AE x 0.43 = Alcohol by Weight

An OG of 12.0 and an AE of 2.0 would yield:
12.0 - 2.0 x 0.43 = 4.3 Alcohol w/w

You can also figure the real extract of beer: take the apparent extract and add the alcohol by weight multiplied by 0.46. This shows the approximate real extract (the actual amount of solids in the beer). Apparent extract is lower because the alcohol lowers the specific gravity.

Apparent Extract + (Alcohol by Weight x 0.46) = Real Extract

For example: AE + (Alcohol w/w x 0.46) = RE

An AE of 2.0 and alcohol of 4.3 (from the example
above) would yield:

2.0 + (4.3 x 0.46) = 3.98 **Real Extract**

You can even use the saccharometer and these
formulas to figure the calories in beer. Take the real
extract and multiply it by 14, then add the alcohol
by weight multiplied by 24. To this, add approximately 5 for the protein in an adjunct brew and 8
in an all-malt brewery, and you have the approximate calories. (These calculations use rule-of-
thumb constants, but are accurate within 5 percent
in virtually all cases.)

(Real Extract x 14) + (Alcohol by Weight x 24) + 5.0 = Calories

(3.98 x 14) + (4.3 x 24) + 5 = 164 **calories**

From this you see that a saccharometer is a very
useful tool. You can figure the original gravity, the
apparent extract, the real extract, and the calories of
beer. But of these, the apparent extract is what really identifies the malt that you sense in your mouth.
Apparent extract is the amount of extract in the
beer (i.e., the real extract) modified by the amount
of alcohol. The more dextrins and sugars in the
beer, the higher the apparent extract; the higher
the alcohol, the lower the apparent extract. It is a
result of those two factors.

I have analyzed almost thirty beers for a number
of characteristics, including the relationship between
the apparent extract and bitterness. This relationship
is crucial for understanding the structure of beer flavor, but I can't support my statement with data here
since the data is proprietary information.

There is a strong relationship between apparent
extract and International Bitterness Units: beers

have a characteristic structure. Within the universe of lagers (I don't know about ales), there is a very characteristic set of relationships between apparent extract and IBUs. I have observed that 80 to 90 percent of the beers sold in America are all within a very limited range, particularly with respect to apparent extract of 10 to 15 IBUs and below 2.5 percent apparent extract. These are the premium beers: the Buds, Millers, Stroh's, Coors, Special Exports, and the light beers.

Then when Americans want something different, they drink Corona or Molson (around 2.2 percent apparent extract and 15 IBUs), which have a little more body and a little more bitterness. Some brewers keep the same amount of body, but do up the bitterness scale, like Heineken or the Beck's beer sold in the U.S. (approximately the same apparent extract, but 20 to 25 IBUs). Beck's German version is very different. This category, together with the first category, is probably 97 percent of the beer consumed in this country.

You also have to remember that the beer recipes in the American breweries evolve. My grandfather worked for one of today's major breweries, and his job was to slightly reformulate the beers every couple of years. This has been true for fifty years, and the latest incident was when several major breweries had a problem with the hops supply last year.

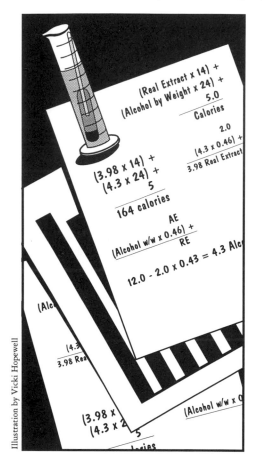

Samuel Adams is very similar to Pilsner Urquell (at over 30 IBUs and over 4.0 percent apparent extract), since my family came from not too far from Pilsen. The classic Pilsener style is very distinctive with high malt content and high bitterness, which is why Michael Jackson noted that its firm malt body was almost southern despite its northern Germany origin. The German Beck's is also very close in style (about 3.5 percent apparent extract and 30 IBUs). In northern Germany, there are different styles that are drier and more bitter tasting, including the Dortmund style (at least 25 to 30 IBUs but 2.5 to 3.0 percent apparent extract) — a beer with less malt body, but about the same amounts of hops.

In analyzing bitterness and body, you can see the difference in American and European tastes in beer. The European tastes run from Carlsberg (less apparent extract than Bud or Miller, but about 20 IBUs) to Pilsner Urquell. American tastes run from Miller Light to Corona and the American Lowenbrau — much lower bitterness and only somewhat malt taste.

Of course, Guinness Extra Stout is off the chart, with its IBU of more than 50. The only way it can carry that level of bitterness is with a lot of black malt, which gives a sweetness that is not visible when you're analyzing apparent extract.

People ask about water and how it fits into beer formulation. As long as water is clean, pure, and with the right mineral content, it isn't a major factor. Budweiser, for instance, makes the same beer from Tampa, Florida water, as it does from water from the Mississippi or the Merrimack rivers, or even from Newark water. Water is most important in your advertising, less important in brewing.

KNOW YOUR CONSUMER THROUGH TESTING

MORTEN C. MEILGAARD, D.SC., F.I. BREW.

C onsumer testing was embraced by all of the large North American brewers when in the early 1970s Miller Brewing Company demonstrated its utility by uncovering the enormous market potential in low-calorie beer. A low-calorie product, Gablinger's — produced by Meister Brau — had been on the market for years, but sales remained low because it was marketed as a diet beer. Miller found through its market research that what millions of consumers wanted was a beer they could drink more of. Miller went to Muncie, Ind., where Gablinger's was a hot brand, and interviewed the men there. Miller found that they bought Gablinger's because it could deliver alcohol and refreshment but was not filling. The Muncians were not afraid of putting on weight — or that was not their stated reason; what the lower calories in Gablinger's did was legitimize the claim that the beer was "less filling."

The rest is history: Miller bought Meister Brau, and today the successor to Gablinger's — Lite — is the world's second best selling brand; now, 40 percent of all beer sold in the United States is low-caloric. Today, consumer-testing activity increases every year as brewers seek to surpass each other in knowledge about their consumers.

REASONS FOR CONDUCTING CONSUMER TESTS

PRODUCT MAINTENANCE

Brewers devote a major proportion of their sensory testing to the maintenance of current products and their market shares and sales volumes. Many of these tests are done by resident panels, but not infrequently a change in raw materials, a process or formulation turns out to be detectable by the panel and must be taken to the consumer. The test is designed to show whether it has a positive or negative effect on preference vs. the competition. For example, it may be found that an expensive method of reducing air content does increase product shelf life. A test is then designed to determine to what extent three-month-old beer treated this way is preferred over regular production

PRODUCT IMPROVEMENT
AND OPTIMIZATION

A product improvement project generally seeks to upgrade one or a few product attributes that consumers have indicated need some improvement. For example, a low-calorie beer may have a grainy or scratchy character compared with regular beer in which this is covered by dextrins. A product optimization project typically manipulates a few ingredients or process variables in an attempt to find a combination that results in a higher level of acceptability vis-à-vis the competition. For example, several levels of malt/adjunct ratio may be tested in order to improve drinkability without losing the overall flavor level.

In product improvement, prototypes are brewed, then tested by a descriptive panel to verify that the desired attribute has been measurably altered. If it has, the prototype is consumer tested to determine the degree of improvement and its effect on overall acceptance or preference scores.

In product optimization, the brewery panel is used to select two or four versions that show measurable sensory differences. Consumer tests are then conducted to determine if consumers perceive the change in attributes and if such modifications improve preference ratings over the competition. Studies such as these enable the company to build up an understanding of those attributes and/or process variables that "drive" overall preference in the market.

DEVELOPMENT OF NEW PRODUCTS

Consumer tests may be useful at several points of the new product cycle. Once a product type is selected, prototypes are sometimes taken to central location tests for confirmation that the desired characteristics survive into large-scale production and to confirm or review the effect on consumers. Finally one or a few versions of the finished product are compared in home placement tests against the competition to firm up the evaluation and serve as justification for the effort and expense of marketing the new product.

If tests do not show the expected and hoped-for advantage over the competition, the test cycle may start over again. Alternatively, if only one or a few attributes need fixing, the project may take on the form of an improvement/optimization effort.

ASSESSMENT OF MARKET POTENTIAL

Frequently a company wishes to examine the market potential in a new area for an existing or a new product. If focus groups show promise, they will be followed by central location tests or by home placement tests.

CATEGORY REVIEW

A category review is undertaken when a company wishes to study the position of its brand or brands within the competitive set, or it may be carried out for the purpose of identifying areas within a product category where opportunities may exist. Typically the process begins with a descriptive analysis by an experienced panel of a set or array of brands and/or prototypes chosen to define or cover the category. Multivariate analysis of the results is used to construct a category map, on which both products and their attributes can be displayed in graph form. This permits researchers to learn the following:

• how products and attributes cluster within the product/attribute space,

• where the opportunities might be in that space for new products, and

• which attributes best define which products.

A requirement for a category review is that the tasters all use the same terminology, which means naive consumers cannot be used. However, it is unproductive to design new products solely for professional panelists; tests must be made with consumers. Two ways of doing this have been proposed (Meilgaard[1]); one is Free Choice Profiling[2] and the other, described by Moskowitz and Jacobs[3], consists of a series of five- to eight-hour sessions using 30 to 100 consumers who spend the first part of the session coming to agreement on a common terminology.

PRINCIPAL METHODS
OF CONSUMER TESTING

Consumer tests, like other sensory tests, can be done professionally in innumerable ways; however, in practice a small number of these have become accepted as the usual methods, giving the user the advantage of being able to compare the results of several studies, interchange results with others, etc. Focus groups, focus panels and one-on-one interviews are qualitative techniques that are relatively inexpensive. Central location tests and home placement tests are quantitative and expensive.

FOCUS GROUPS

Focus groups[4] are a technique for getting ideas and detecting emerging trends towards acceptance or rejection of particular product ideas. Focus groups are useful for determining the extent of consumer knowledge, consumer terminology and getting at the "why's" of consumer attitudes.

Typically, ten to twelve consumers selected on the basis of specific criteria — for example, male, legal age to thirty-five, having purchased imported beer twice or more in the past month — meet for a one- to two-hour session with the focus group moderator. The moderator plays a key role in presenting the subject of interest and facilitating the discussion using group dynamics techniques to uncover as much specific information as possible about the focus of the session.

Typically, two or three such sessions are held with different participants, but with the same project focus. At the end, the moderator provides a summary of the results.

A purist will say that three groups of twelve, that is, thirty-six verdicts are too few to be representative of a consumer trend or the validity of a new product idea. But in practice, trends often emerge that do make sense, and focus group moderators become sought after and command high fees if they can elicit good ideas or spot authentic trends. The key is identifying and understanding the trend; the small group will not reveal the extent of the trend.

FOCUS PANELS

In this variant of the focus group, the interviewer utilizes the same group of consumers two or three more times, i.e., they become a panel. The objective is to make initial contact with the group, have discussion on the topic, send the group home to use the product at home or at a party, and then have the group return to discuss its experiences.

ONE-ON-ONE INTERVIEWS

In-depth, one-on-one interviews are designed to elicit specific information too detailed to be collected in a focus group or focus panel setting. The interviewer conducts successive interviews with as many as fifty consumers, using the same format with each, but probing in response to each consumer's answers. For example, the sponsor may be looking for ideas for entirely new beer products using fruit juices, or he may with to evaluate sensitive questions to which people in a group would give a stock response, for example beer types and situations of use uniquely suited for women.

CENTRAL LOCATION TESTS

As the name indicates, these are tests carried out at a shopping mall, bar, hotel, community hall, fair, or exhibition where people can be waylaid for ten or twenty minutes to test a product and answer questions. Synonyms are mall intercept tests and hall tests. The organizers accost persons who are then "screened," i.e., asked a set of questions aimed at determining whether or not they fulfill the agreed criteria. The selected respondents are taken to the booth, asked a set of questions regarding their age, occupation, income group, beer consumption habits, etc., then given the test, which typically consists of testing two, three or four beers and filling in a questionnaire describing their impressions and preferences. A typical central location test set comprises three to five locations representing different sales areas, and 50 to 200 respondents per location.

The advantages of central location tests are that results can be collected from many screened respondents in a short time, and that the organizers have full control of the condition of the product and the glasses etc. The major disadvantage is that the "sip" format is an unreliable predictor of preference for most U.S. beers, for which a greater volume of consumption is needed. Again, many people, not being accustomed to taste testing, are somewhat out of their depth in the unfamiliar situation of a booth where someone is waiting for a form to be completed, hence they tend to be distracted, and findings may contain a major proportion of poorly considered or haphazard verdicts.

HOME PLACEMENT TESTS

Respondents are screened, and those selected typically receive a six-pack of one product at a time, with instructions to call the organizer when it is used up and the scoresheet filled in, so that the next product can be delivered. The reason for not providing two or more products for comparison is the opportunity this would offer for using the wrong clues as the basis of revaluation, or for assigning responses to the wrong scoresheet. Typical panel sizes are 75 to 300 per city in three or four cities.

Home placement tests often represent the ultimate stage in consumer testing. The product is tested under normal conditions of use, both physically and psychologically. Discrimination and reliability are improved because opinions can be stabilized from repeated testing rather than being based on a first sip. Because more time is available for the completion of the scoresheet, more information can be collected regarding the consumer's purchasing habits and his or her attitudes to other than sensory characteristics of the product, e.g., packaging, price, situation of use, etc. Disadvantages are that tests are costly and take a minimum of three to four weeks to carry out. A maximum of three samples can be compared; thus multi-sample tests such as optimization and category review cannot be carried out by home placement.

PRACTICAL CONSIDERATIONS

It is not unusual to hear brewers complain that brand decisions based on consumer testing have turned out to be wrong more often than they were accurate, and to argue that one would have been much better off by listening to experienced brewers and people in the trade, who have their ear to the ground.

In this reviewer's experience, some consumer tests have indeed yielded the wrong advice, but so have some of the experienced people. The best course must be to continue to use both, but to refine one's techniques and learn from one's errors as experience is accumulated.

CHOICE OF TEST SUBJECTS

The first requirement is that the test subjects truly represent the intended market, i.e., they should be a truly random and proportional selection of the intended customer group. For a widely consumed product such as a nationally distributed beer, this would require thousands of test subjects; in practice, cost considerations usually limit the number to 200 to 1,200, and some compromises are necessary. Among the considerations used in choosing the subjects are:

Usage This may include light, moderate and heavy users of the products of interest, or the specific usage such as "users of one six-pack per week or more."

Age Most studies assume (perhaps unjustly) that beer drinkers choose their brands before a certain age and that any switching done later is small in comparison and less rewarding to study. Hence, most protocols specify "Legal age to twenty-five," "Legal age to thirty-five," or "Legal age to forty-nine," the latter for nonalcoholic and low-alcohol beer.

Sex Even though as much as a quarter of all beer is consumed by women, men dominate the choice of brand; unless the product investigated is specifically for women, the protocol will specify "male."

Income Protocols for studies of beer generally ignore income as a criterion for selection of test subjects.

Geographic location This is so important that the large majority of studies select three to six locations across the United States. In Texas, both beer and glass must be ice cold, bitterness must be low, and foam is not a consideration; more than 60 percent of beer is low-calorie. In the Northeast, beer must have bitterness and foam and should be flavorful and hoppy.

| Ethnic group | The protocol should include blacks and Hispanics as each are 10 to 15 percent of the U.S. population. |

Education, employment, marital status Usually not specified.

DESIGN OF QUESTIONNAIRE
The main considerations are:

| **Length** | Usually one wants to ask more questions than can be accommodated. Experienced organizers keep the length in proportion to the time the subject expects to be in the test situation and limit the questions essential to achieving the project objective. |

Questions about the respondent Essential questions in most cases are sex, age, ethnic group, education and occupation.

Questions about the test products (See examples.) The main question regarding preference, acceptance or purchase intent may be placed first on the scoresheet; however, in cases where a consumer is asked several specific questions about appearance and aroma before the actual consumption of the product, it is necessary to wait until those attributes are evaluated and rated before addressing the total acceptance or preference question. Preference may be stated either by ranking or means of a hedonic scale such as a "just right" scale.[5] Next, the questioner attempts to probe the respondent's reasons for the verdict. Space is always left open for spontaneous remarks; in addition, the respondent may be asked to rate each product on a series of attribute scales of the type (too little ——— too much); e.g., for freshness, fullness, smoothness and bitterness.

Vocabulary	A major problem is that the typical consumer knows only the above terms plus sour, sweet and salty, while the difference between samples may reside in attributes such as hop aroma, estery or fruity bouquet, worty or grainy notes, etc. Each major brewing company has developed its own way around this obstacle, and this is one of the closely guarded secrets of the profession. One method is to hold focus group sessions in which the participants are taught to recognize the attributes of interest, but this is a double-edged sword as many will switch preference towards more "hoppy," "estery," "fruity," etc. in order to appear sophisticated in front of the group. Newspaper-sponsored taste tests in the United States almost invariably give highest marks to bitter and heavily flavored beers, which the panel members would rarely choose on their own.

PROTOCOL DESIGN

A test protocol is a detailed description agreed beforehand between the brewer and the test organizer. Among the items it must contain are:

Test facility	The location should provide adequate space and privacy for each consumer/subject and the necessary number of test administrators and helpers. It should have proper lighting, temperature, noise control, odor control, and space for product handling and glass washing.
Test administrators	The administrators are required to be both trained and experienced in the specific type of test design to be used. A detailed set of instructions must be developed for the handling of questionnaires, subjects and samples.
Test subjects	The protocol specifies the criteria for selection and a "screener" is developed. Once selected, subjects are

made aware of the location, type and number of products to be tested, approximate time required, and remuneration, if any. Test subjects do not respond well to surprises regarding what is expected of them.

Sample screening The protocol details how the test samples are to be screened in advance of the test to determine, for example, exact samples to be tested, storage conditions under which each sample is to be held and shipped; packaging requirements for storage and shipping; shipping method (air, truck, refrigerated, etc.); and descriptive analysis by the company panel to document the sensory characteristics of the samples at the time they are used in the test.

Sample handling As part of the test protocol, instructions are detailed regarding receipt, storage, handling, preparation and presentation of samples at the test site.

Validation As a guarantee against sloppy workmanship by local test administrators, typically 15 percent of the respondents are called by telephone after the session, by a different company, to ascertain that they were indeed tested and to obtain their impressions of the event.

DATA ANALYSIS

This important part of the test may consist of the following:

Totals For each question asked, the total of points or votes awarded by, first, all respondents and second, by each group of respondents; e.g., male, age, ethnic group, city, education, consumption group (low/medium/high), those who answered yes/no to a certain question, etc.

Mean number of responses on which based, and the standard deviation.

Multivariate statistical analysis Consumer tests often yield data sets containing numerous variables measured on each of a number of samples; hence they offer wide scope for multivariate analysis techniques. Discussion of multivariate techniques is outside the scope of this paper; see Meilgaard et al.[6] for a basic review of the above techniques, with examples; a number of more sophisticated applications can be found in the proceedings of two recent symposia.[7,8]

OPPORTUNITIES AND PITFALLS

Here are some things North American brewers have learned by consumer testing. As this is a very secretive area, in fact the most secret in all of brewing, what follows is of necessity much colored by subjective guesswork rather than objective fact.

Consumers can taste small differences. In home placement tests, consumers fall only slightly behind experienced panels; for example, where a panel may detect a difference in bitterness of 2 BU, consumers can detect 3 BU.

Consumers have virtually no flavor vocabulary and cannot remember flavors other than sweet, sour, salt, and bitter, and even these only imperfectly. In a specific test, only one out of 300 mentioned hops when comparing a strongly hopped aromatic beer with an unhopped control. When comparing two beers of which one contained 20 ppm added isohumulone, 100 percent of the panel could taste the difference, but only 10 percent circled "bitter" while 70 percent circled "stronger" or other terms.

Consumers do remember a bad experience, even thought they cannot put a name to it. In the long run, only those brands survive that have a low incidence of bad beer and a zero incidence of visible faults such as haze or particles.

Consumers "drink the label rather than the beer." This well-known theory has been confirmed again and again: purchase decisions are based not on flavor but on what the consumer believes he or she ought to be seen consuming. Young men on a date order low-calorie beer, not because they like its flavor, but because women give preference to a man who is seen to pace himself.

Brand user image operates separately from "flavor" and is a function of advertising and promotion activities.

Product image counts. The same beer will "taste better" when one knows that it was difficult and expensive to brew, and when it is poured from a package of appealing design and label graphics. Today's "cold-filtered" beers cannot be distinguished by a panel from the pasteurized version, yet people buy them because it is known that they are harder to make.

Beer drinking is not an event, it is a process. Mostly beer is consumed when one is doing something; only 5 percent is consumed sipwise at a cafe, the rest with friends at a game or barbecue, on a sailboat, at a picnic or dance, etc. thus, the flavor and satiation should not be so prominent that the beer gets in the way of the main activity.

ULTRALIGHT BEER: TEST BREW

Instructions
This product was brewed for use when a really light beer is needed, for example after sports on a hot afternoon. The alcohol is 2/3 of regular light beer. Drink as much as you like, then place one mark in each category below:

Color   ○ ○ ○ ○ ○ ○
too light   too dark

Foam   ○ ○ ○ ○ ○ ○
too little   too much

Fullness   ○ ○ ○ ○ ○ ○
too thin   too full

Freshness   ○ ○ ○ ○ ○ ○
stale/not fresh   very fresh

Alcohol   ○ ○ ○ ○ ○ ○
too little   too much

Taste   ○ ○ ○ ○ ○ ○
unpleasant   pleasant

Overall evaluation:

○ ○ ○ ○ ○ ○ ○ ○ ○

| Like extremely | Like very much | Like moderately | Like slightly | Neither like nor dislike | Dislike slightly | Dislike moderately | Dislike very much | Dislike extremely |

Comments _____

_____

_____

Name _____**Date**_____

SCREENER — PLACEMENT
Beer Home Use Test

Circle Age Group:
1 Legal age to 25   2 26-35

Circle City:
1 Sacramento, CA   2 Rochester, MN   3 Boston, MA   4 Jacksonville, FL

Respondent's Name _____Telephone (   ) _____

Address _____City _____State _____Zipcode _____

Interviewer's Name _____I.D.# _____Time Begun_____a.m./p.m.

Date _____Time Ended_____a.m./p.m.

Approach Males Aged 21-34 Years

"Hello, I'm_____from XXXYYY, Inc., a national market research firm. We're conducting a survey in this area".

Interviewer: All questions should be asked as stated. All responses are to be recorded verbatim.

1. "Do you or any member of your family work for a(n) _____

(Read list)	**Yes**	**No**
Advertising Agency	1	2
Market Research Firm	1	2
Company involved with the production or distribution of alcoholic beverages	1	2
The military service?"	1	2

If any 1 circled, terminate, record on tally sheet, erase and re-use.

2. "Have you participated in a consumer research study in this shopping mall within the past three months?"

Yes   1   *(Terminate, record on tally sheet, erase and re-use)*
No   2   *(continue)*

3. *(Hand respondent age card)* "Please look at this card and tell me the letter that corresponds to your age." *(Check I.D. of anyone 25 or younger or who looks to be of questionable age)*

Under legal age	1	*(terminate, record on tally sheet, erase and re-use)*
Legal age to 25	2	*(eligible for legal to 25 quota)*
26 to 35	3	*(eligible for 26-35 quota)*
36 to 45	4	
46 to 55	5	*(terminate, record on tally sheet, erase and re-use)*
56 and over	6	

4. "Which of the following beverages have you drunk during the past week, either at home or away from home?" *(Read list, circle all that apply)*

Carbonated soft drinks 1
Milk 2
Beer 3   *If 3 not circled, terminate, record on*
Wine 4   *tally sheet, erase and re-use*

---

5. "How many cans, bottles or glasses of beer do you drink in a typical week? Please be sure to consider those you drink at home and away from home." *(Record exact number below)*

#_____ *(If less than 6, terminate, record on tally sheet, erase and re-use)*

---

6. "Do you have a phone at home?"
Yes 1
No 2

---

7. "A leading producer of beer would like to obtain your opinions of 2 beers. We would like to give you 2 different sixpacks of beer to use at home during the next 6 days. After that we will be calling to get your opinions. Would you be willing to participate in this test?"

Yes 1   *(continue)*
No 2   *(Terminate, record on tally sheet, erase and re-use)*

---

8. "Before I give you the products, I'd like to ask you a few questions about beer in general. First, I'd like to ask you about the brands of beer you drink."

For questions 8, 9 and 10, record answers on sheet A. If respondent answers any of the starred brands, please ask him: "Is that the (brand) light or regular?"

"Which one brand of beer would you say you drink most often?"
(Do not read sheet A. Record one answer under Q.8)

---

9. "What other brands of beer do you drink regularly?" *(Do not read sheet A. Record brands under Q.9). (Probe)* "Any other brands?" *(Continue probing until no other brands mentioned).*

---

10. "Are there other brands of beer that you have tried in the past month?" *(If yes, ask:)* "What are they?" *(Do not read sheet A. Record under Q. 10). (Probe)* "Any other brands?" *(Continue probing until no other brands mentioned).*

11. "We would now like to give you two six-packs of beer to take home." *(Hand respondent 1 sixpack of beer #_____ "Use first" and 1 sixpack of beer #_____ "Use second". Place both in a handled shopping bag).* "Drink these as you would normally drink beer. However, please be sure you are the only person to drink the products. Place the sixpack labeled #_____ "Use First" in the refrigerator for at least 12 hours before drinking. We will call you in 3 days to get your opinions".

"Please be sure not to place the sixpack labeled #_____ "Use Second" in the refrigerator or drink it until after we call you to get your opinion of the first sixpack."

....

12. "Now, before you leave I would like to make an appointment with you to get your opinions of the first six-pack 3 days from today. When would be the best time for me to call? (Make appointment 3 days from today")."

Day	Date	Time

March

S	M	T	W	T	F	S
1	2	3	4	5	6	7
8	9	10	11	12	13	14
15	16	17	18	19	20	21
22	23	24	25	26	27	28
29	30	31				

....

13. Interviewer: Record respondent's race.

Black _____ 1
White _____ 2
Other _____ 3 (Specify)_____

CONCLUSIONS

The use of consumer tests is increasing in North America because more and more, beer is consumed for reasons apart from or in addition to its flavor, i.e., for qualities that cannot be determined by a descriptive panel. Those reasons can often be discovered with the aid of focus groups and one-on-one interviews. Confirmation that a brand is suitable for the market is then obtained via central location tests or preferably, by home placement tests.

ACKNOWLEDGMENTS

The author is grateful to the Stroh Brewery Company for use of its facilities and for the permission to publish this paper. Thanks are due to E.A. Benfield of the marketing department for information and helpful discussion.

REFERENCES

[1] Meilgaard, M.C. "Current progress in sensory analysis." A review. *Journal of the American Society of Brewing Chemists* 49, 101-109, 1991.

[2] Oreskovich, D.C., Klein, B.P. & Sutherland, J.W. "Procrustes analysis and its applications to Free-Choice and other sensory profiling." *Sensory Science, Theory and Application in Foods.* H.T. Lawless and B.P. Klein, Eds., Marcel Dekker, New York 1991, 353-393.

[3] Moskowitz, H.R. & Jacobs, B.E. *Product Testing with Consumers for Research Guidance.* L.S. Wu, Ed., Standard Technical Publication No. 1035, Philadelphia: American Society for Testing and Materials, 1989, 64-74.

[4] Krueger, R.A. *Focus Groups: A Practical Guide for Applied Research. Newbury Park*, CA 19320, Sage Publications, 1988, 197 pp.

[5] Chambers IV, E. & Smith, E.A. "The uses of qualitative research in product research and development." *Sensory Science: Theory and Applications in Foods*. H.T. Lawless & B.P. Klein, Eds., Marcel Dekker, New York 9191, 395-412.

[6] Meilgaard, M.C., Civille, G.C. & Carr, B.T., *Sensory Evaluation Techniques*, 2nd Edition, Boca Raton, Florida: CRC Press, 1991, Chapter 12.

[7] Wu, L.S., Ed., *Product Testing with Consumers for Research Guidance*. Standard Technical Publication No. 1035., Philadelphia: American Society for Testing and Materials, 1989, 90 pp.

[8] Piggott, J.R., Ed., Statistical Procedures in Food Research. London: Elsevier Applied Science, 1986, 412 pp.

AROMA IDENTIFICATION
FOLLOWED BY BEER FLAVOR TERMINOLOGY CHART
BY MORTEN C. MEILGAARD, D.SC., F.I. BREW.

CHARLIE PAPAZIAN & GREGORY NOONAN

Before we taste beer, our olfactory receptors perceive the aroma of beer. That aroma plays a very important part in how we evaluate beer's flavor. The standards for aroma identification are based on the reference standards specified by Dr. Morton Meilgaard of the Stroh Brewing Company. Dr. Meilgaard has done years and years of research on flavor and aroma evaluation. He led the joint American Society of Brewing Chemists and the European Brewing Congress Subcommittee on Sensory Analysis in the identification of major sensory stimulants in beer, and he developed a Beer Flavor Terminology System supported by appropriate reference standards (see page 208).

Only by training our olfactory sense and taste buds to recognize particular smells and tastes and to identify these by specific terms can we, as judges, beer evaluators, brewers, and beer drinkers, ever hope to communicate to one another something specific about our likes and dislikes of a given brew.

When you begin to understand what Dr. Meilgaard and his associates have made possible, you can really appreciate how valuable this information is. For example, in one study that is indicative of the training it takes to understand what flavor and aroma are about, a group of university students, 14 percent mistakenly identified citric acid as "bitter" and 8 percent called quinine sulfate in solution "sour," although it is very bitter. That is like telling somebody whose house is painted red, that it is yellow. We communicate better with our sense of sight, but our senses of smell and taste are often taken for granted.

As beer evaluators, particularly if you are involved with judging beer, you understand that you taste certain things in beer. Yet, how do you communicate that flavor? If someone says a beer tastes of dimethyl sulfide (DMS) does he mean to say it has a skunky flavor? Or is he really talking about a sulfury or winy character? Knowing how to make those identifications of flavor or aroma takes practice.

The Beer Flavor Terminology System enables us to relate beer identification terms to sensations, giving us a common language framework within which to communicate about beer and point out ways for us to improve our beer. The work that has produced this system, is no small accomplishment. Isolating major stimulants — in all, 120 of them in fourteen classes — involves resolving regional and even international semantic disparities, investigating, identifying, testing, and accepting or rejecting possible standards. It includes establishing threshold sensitivity and appropriate standard concentration for these compounds.

As an indication of its importance, I would like to point out that the American Society of Enology and Viticulture has adopted Dr. Meilgaard's work in a Wine Aroma Wheel and standardized Wine Aroma Terminology and Standards. *Malting and Brewing Science*, a technical book on brewing, devotes pages to it, and it is often referred to in other publications, magazines, and journals. It is as useful a tool as any piece of brewing equipment.

Why is this so? Because for the most part, smell is an untrained sense. The ability to smell

odors is incredibly acute. Humans can smell minute concentrations of aromatic compounds, often in as little as parts per billion. If we are trained to recognize specific aromas, and to relate those to brewing processes or ingredients, we can correct deficiencies in our beer's flavor and aroma. As judges we can go beyond our likes and dislikes and recognize whether an entry is appropriate or inappropriate within a stylistic category.

There is, however, a correct method for sniffing beer to gain maximum olfactory sensation. In our olfactory sense, there is an olfactory cleft. What I liken it to is a a little pocket that receives molecules of aroma and sends signals to the brain. Evidently, from articles I have read and researched, only about 4 percent of aroma compounds ever reach that cleft. In order to better perceive aromas, it is important to train yourself to sniff at an odor in short sniffs in order to bring more molecules into that area. What I do when I smell a beer is take short strong sniffs and if that doesn't do it, I take strong, deep breaths. I also swirl the glass — that is again another important aspect of gaining maximum aroma for when you swirl the glass, you release the bubbles that carry the aroma into your nose.

In sampling doctored beers, some people will not be able to perceive what others perceive. Some will have "blind spots" to certain smells, particularly the sulfur smells. There are people who are not sensitive to, let's say, sulfur dioxide. You know what sulfur dioxide is; to most of us, it stinks, to say the least, and it even irritates the sinuses. Some people, however, cannot perceive that.

There are circumstances that decrease the sensitivity to odors. For example, if you have a cold, or you are one or two days away from getting a cold, your sense of smell and taste will be affected. Even if you don't feel ill, but you are coming down with the flu or a cold, your sense of flavor and smell can be affected one or two days before you come down with it. Likewise, certain vitamin deficiencies can affect your sensitivity to smell and aroma. Eating certain foods will affect your sensitivity to smell and taste. Some research has shown ingesting alcohol or sugar diminishes your ability to smell. On the other hand, acids and things that are sour or bitter — such as red wine and coffee — can enhance your ability to perceive flavors and aromas.

(For additional information on how to produce beer samples, please see Table 7 on page 72, "Sensory Evaluation for Brewers.")

I would like to caution you, before I tell you about the doctored beers, that these are not to be tasted. They are to be smelled only. Some of the additives in the beers are poisonous. I experimented last week in my home with doctoring some beers, and I must tell you that if you plan to make one of these aroma identification kits, please get written permission from your spouse or roommate first. Some of these odors can lead to dissension. The terrible odors can linger three days or longer. If you are going to put together some samples, find someone who has a laboratory with a good ventilation system. Otherwise you are going to be living with almondy smell, diacetyl or the lacquer thinner smell or ethyl acetate for three days. It isn't pleasant at all.

The other thing that is difficult in putting together these aroma identification kits is that many of these aromas are very volatile and unstable. It is suggested that these concentrations be put into beer samples only twelve to twenty-four hours before they are actually sampled. Otherwise, many of them are so volatile and unstable that their propensities will diminish.

The chart, "Beer Aromas and Their Possible Sources" on page 206 can be very useful to us as brewers as it tells us how we can improve our comments when we evaluate other peoples' beer. As a professional brewer, you should be able to recognize certain flavors or aromas that you may be blind to. You may be making a beer with a strong diacetyl character to it, and if you are blind to that, you will never detect it. That is why all breweries should have a panel of tasters, not just a brewmaster. There are some very competent brewmasters who are blind to diacetyl. The wise ones know they are! It is very important for all brewers, and particularly commercial operations, to have an objective, trained panel to taste and smell the beer. What doctored samples do is to begin that training.

The equipment I used to make these samples was not very sophisticated. I used a pipette, which is a long graduated cylinder. To make a concentration of one part per million, take a sample of your chemical and dilute it one in one hundred milliliters of distilled water. Then dilute one milliliter of that solution into a hundred milliliters of distilled water — that gives you one part in ten thousand. By continuing this dilution process, you can easily get concentrations measurable in parts per million and parts per billion.

Some of the chemicals used to doctor these samples were obtained from chemical companies, others through grocery stores, and household-items stores. Some are not very soluble in water. In that case, I use a capful of grain (ethanol) alcohol in a beaker with the high-concentration solution and dissolve the chemicals in the alcohol before I add the distilled water. Otherwise there are globs of oil floating around.

One word of caution: we have to be careful not to define all of these taste sensations as bad. I believe that if any of these are too strong, then they are bad. In tiny, minute amounts, however, they may add character to an otherwise bland-tasting beer. So in beers where the flavor level is really low, like most mass-produced beers, most of these characteristics may be perceived as bad. In full-flavored brews, however, like the ones you are making, many of these flavor components might very well be desirable.

For example, the clove characteristic — a characteristic of Bavarian wheat beer — is desirable for that style. Diacetyl in American Pilsener style, is not at all appropriate, but in certain styles of ales, particularly English pale ales, a certain amount of that can be very nice. Too much, and you need to figure out ways to cut back on it. DMS is generally a characteristic of most lagers, and at almost imperceptible levels. It adds flavor and aroma that makes a lager a lager. Yet having DMS in an ale may not be appropriate.

Beer Aroma Recognition Guidelines

(Much of this data is from Dr. Morton Meilgaard's work on the subject and Charlie Papazian's experience with handling samples)

Mielgaard Ref. #/ Concentration Descriptor	General Descriptor	Technical for Recognition	Substance Used in 12 oz. beer	Concentration one quart beer
0110 Alcoholic	Alcohol	Ethanol	15 ml	40 ml
0111 Clove	Spicy	Eugenol	40 micrograms	106 mg
		Allspice	2 g	5 g
		Cloves	(marinate cloves in beer)	
0112 Winy	Fusely, Vinous	Gallo Chablis	3 fl. oz.	8 fl. oz.
0123 Solventlike	Acetone	Laquer thinner	0.02 ml	0.05 ml
0133 Estery, Fruity, Solvent	Ethyl Acetate	Ethyl Acetate	0.007 ml or 7 mg	0.019 ml or 7 mg
0150 Green Apples	Acetaldehyde	Acetaldehyde	0.002 ml or 2 mg	0.005 ml or 5 mg
0220 Sherry	Sherry	Sherry	2.5 fl. oz.	6.5 fl. oz.
0224 Almond, Nutty	Nutty	Benzaldehyde	0.002 ml or 2 mg	0.005 ml or 5 mg
		Almond Extract	4 drops	11 drops
0503 Medicinal, Band-Aidlike, Plasticlike	Phenolic	Phenol	0.003 ml or 3 mg	0.01 ml or 10 mg
620 Butter, Butterscotch	Diacetyl	Diacetyl	0.0001 ml or 0.1 mg	0.00027 ml or 0.27 mg
		Butter flavor extract	4 drops	11 drops
0710 Sulfury	Sulfitic, Sulfur dioxide	Sodium or Potassium Metabisulfite	2 mg	5 mg
0721 Skunky, lightstruck	Skunky	Beer exposed to light		
0732 Sweet corn, cabbage	Dimethylsulfide/ DMS	Dimethylsulfide/ DMS (note:unstable)	0.00003 ml or 30 mg	0.0001 ml or 100 mg
0800 Stale, Cardboard	Stale, Oxidation	Heat sample for one week at 90-100 degrees F (32-38 degrees C), or marinate cardboard in beer		
0910 Sour/Vinegar	Acetic (acid)	White Vinegar	30 ml	100 ml
0920 Sour/Lactic	Lactic (acid)	Lactic Acid	0.4 ml	1.1 ml

Note: Some of these substances are poisonous and should not be tasted.

Beer Aromas and Their Possible Sources

0110	Alcoholic	High starting gravity, excessive attenuation
0111	Clove	Characteristic of wheat beer; if excessive, wild-yeast contamination
0112	Winy	From oxidation, except strong lagers or barley wines
0123	Solventlike	From warm fermentation, plastic, wild yeast, common in old estery ales
0133	Estery, Fruity, Solvent	From warm fermentation, yeast strain, too few yeast nutrients
0150	Green Apples	High fermentation temperature, insufficient yeast pitched, beer racked too early
0220	Sherry	Warm fermentation or oxidation, very old beer
0224	Almond, Nutty	Oxidation, very old beer
0503	Medicinal/Phenolic	From water supply, chlorine residue, plastic, wild yeast, improper sparging techniques
0620	Butter/Diacetyl	High initial fermentation temperature, racked, cooled or fined too soon, pediococcus contamination
0710	Sulfury, SO_2	Wild yeast contamination
0721	Skunky	Beer exposed to light
0732	Sweet corn, DMS	Insufficient kettle boil, wort chilled too slowly, coliform bacteria contamination
0800	Stale, cardboard	From oxidation of amino acids during aging, at bottling, in bottle, old beer — heat accelerates the process
0910	Sour vinegar	Acetobacter contamination
0920	Sour-lactic	Lactobacillus contamination

Flavor Wheel

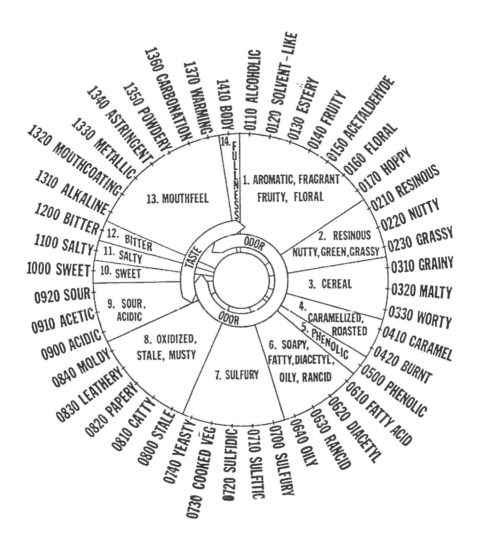

Beer Flavor Terminology Chart by Morten C. Meilgaard, D.Sc., F.I. Brew.

RECOMMENDED DESCRIPTORS

Particular Relevance:
O = Odor   T = Taste   M = Mouthfeel   W = Warming   Af = Afterflavor

Class Term	First Tier	Second Tier	Relevance	Comments, Synonyms, Definitions	Reference Standard
Class 1 — Aromatic, Fragrant, Fruity, Floral					
0110	Alcoholic		OTW	General effect of ethanol and higher alcohols	Ethanol, 50 g/L
0111		Spicy	OTW	Allspice, nutmeg, peppery, eugenol; see also 1003 Vanilla	Eugenol, 120 µg/L
0112		Vinous	OTW	Bouquet, fusely, winelike	(White wine)
0120	Solventlike		OT	Like chemical solvents	
0121		Plastics	OT	Plasticizers	
0122		Can-liner	OT	Lacquerlike	
0123		Acetone	OT		(Acetone)
0130	Estery		OT	Like aliphatic esters	
0131		Isoamyl acetate	OT	Banana, peardrop	(Isoamyl acetate)
0132		Ethyl hexanoate	OT	Applelike with note of aniseed; see also 0142 Apple	(Ethyl hexanoate)
0133		Ethyl acetate	OT	Light fruity, solventlike; see also 0120 Solventlike	
0140	Fruity		OT	Of specific fruits or mixtures of fruits	
0141		Citrus	OT	Citral, grapefruit, lemony, orange rind	
0142		Apple	OT		
0143		Banana	OT		
0144		Black currant	OT	Black currant fruit; for black currant leaves use 0810 Catty	
0145		Melony	OT		(6-Nonenal, *cis-* or *trans-*)
0146		Pear	OT		

Class Term	First Tier	Second Tier	Rele-vance	Comments, Synonyms, Definitions	Reference Standard
		0147 Raspberry	OT		
		0148 Strawberry	OT		
	0150 Acetaldehyde		OT	Green apples, raw apple skin, bruised apples	(Acetaldehyde)
	0160 Floral		OT	Like flowers, fragrant	
		0161 2-Phenylethanol	OT	Roselike	(2-Phenylethanol)
		0162 Geraniol	OT	Roselike, different from 0161; taster should compare pure chemicals	(Geraniol)
		0163 Perfumy	OT	Scented	(Exaltolide musk)
	0170 Hoppy		OT	Fresh hop aroma; use with other terms to describe stale hop aroma; does not include hop bitterness (see 1200 Bitter)	
		0171 Kettle-hop	OT	Flavor imparted by aroma hops boiled in kettle	
		0172 Dry-hop	OT	Flavor imparted by dry hops added in tank or cask	
		0173 Hop oil	OT	Flavor imparted by addition of distilled hop oil	

Class 2 — Resinous, Nutty, Green, Grassy

Class Term	First Tier	Second Tier	Rele-vance	Comments, Synonyms, Definitions	Reference Standard
	0210 Resinous		OT	Fresh sawdust, resin, cedarwood, pinewood, sprucy, terpenoid	
		0211 Woody	OT	Seasoned wood (uncut)	
	0220 Nutty		OT	As in brazil nut, hazelnut, sherrylike	
		0221 Walnut	OT	Fresh (not rancid) walnut	
		0222 Coconut	OT		
		0223 Beany	OT	Bean soup	(2,4,7-Decatrienal)
		0224 Almond	OT	Marzipan	(Benzaldehyde)
	0230 Grassy		OT		
		0231 Freshly cut grass	OT	Green, crushed green leaves, leafy, alfalfa	(cis-3-Hexenol)
		0232 Strawlike	OT	Haylike	

Class Term	First Tier	Second Tier	Relevance	Comments, Synonyms, Definitions	Reference Standard
Class 3 — Cereal					
	0310 Grainy		OT	Raw grain flavor	
		0311 Husky	OT	Husklike, chaff, *Glattwasser*	
		0312 Corn grits	OT	Maize grits, adjuncty	
		0313 Mealy	OT	Like flour	
	0320 Malty		OT		
	0330 Worty		OT	Fresh wort aroma; use with other terms to describe infected wort (e.g.: 0731 Parsnip/celery)	
Class 4 — Caramelized, Roasted					
	0410 Caramel		OT	Burnt sugar, toffeelike	
		0411 Molasses	OT	Black treacle, treacly	
		0412 Licorice	OT		
	0420 Burnt		OTM	Scorched aroma, dry mouthfeel, sharp, acrid taste	
		0421 Bread crust	OTM	Charred toast	
		0422 Roast barley	OTM	Chocolate malt	
		0423 Smoky	OT		
Class 5 — Phenolic					
0500 Phenolic			OT		
		0501 Tarry	OT	Pitch, faulty pitching of containers	
		0502 Bakelite	OT		
		0503 Carbolic	OT	Phenol, C_6H_5OH	
		0504 Chlorophenol	OT	Trichlorophenol (TCP), hospitallike	
		0505 Iodoform	OT	Iodophors, hospitallike, pharmaceutical	

Class 6 — Soapy, Fatty, Diacetyl, Oily, Rancid

Class Term	First Tier	Second Tier	Relevance	Comments, Synonyms, Definitions	Reference Standard
	0610 Fatty acid		OT		
		0611 Caprylic	OT	Soapy, fatty, goaty, tallowy	(Octanoic acid)
		0612 Cheesy	OT	Dry, stale cheese, old hops ⎫ Hydroytic rancidity	(Isovaleric acid)
		0613 Isovaleric	OT	⎬	Butyric acid, 3 mg/L
		0614 Butyric	OT	Rancid butter ⎭	
	0620 Diacetyl		OT	Butterscotch, buttermilk	Diacetyl, 0.2-0.4 mg/L
	0630 Rancid		OT		
		0631 Rancid oil	OTM	Oxidative rancidity	
	0640 Oily		OTM		
		0641 Vegetable oil	OTM	As in refined vegetable oil	
		0642 Mineral oil	OTM	Gasoline (petrol), kerosene (paraffin), machine oil	

Class 7 — Sulfury

Class Term	First Tier	Second Tier	Relevance	Comments, Synonyms, Definitions	Reference Standard
0700 Sulfury					
	0710 Sulfitic		OT	Sulfur dioxide, striking match, choking, sulfurous-SO_2	(KMS)
	0720 Sulfidic		OT	Rotten egg, sulfury-reduced, sulfurous-RSH	
		0721 H_2S	OT	Rotten egg	(H_2S)
		0722 Mercaptan	OT	Lower mercaptans, drains, stench	(Ethyl Mercaptan)
		0723 Garlic	OT		
		0724 Lightstruck	OT	Skunky, sunstruck	
		0725 Autolysed	OT	Rotting yeast; see also 0740 Yeasty	
		0726 Burnt rubber	OT	Higher mercaptans	
		0727 Shrimplike	OT	Water in which shrimp have been cooked	

Class Term	First Tier	Second Tier	Relevance	Comments, Synonyms, Definitions	Reference Standard
		0730 Cooked vegetable	OT	Mainly dialkyl sulfides, sulfurous-RSR	
		0731 Parsnip, Celery	OT	Effect of wort infection	
		0732 DMS	OT	(Dimethyl sulfide)	DMS 100 µg/L
		0733 Cooked cabbage	OT	Overcooked green vegetables	
		0734 Cooked sweet corn	OT	Cooked maize, canned sweet corn	
		0735 Cooked tomato	OT	Tomato juice (processed), tomato ketchup	
		0736 Cooked onion	OT		
		0740 Yeasty	OT	Fresh yeast, flavor of heated thiamine; see also 0725 Autolysed	
		0741 Meaty	OT	Brothy, cooked meat, meat extract, peptone, yeast broth.	

Class 8 — Oxidized, Stale, Musty

Class Term	First Tier	Second Tier	Relevance	Comments, Synonyms, Definitions	Reference Standard
0800 Stale			OTM	Old beer, overaged, overpasteurized	(Heat with air)
	0810 Catty		OT	Black currant leaves, ribes, tomato plants, oxidized beer	(p-Methane-8-thiol-3-one)
	0820 Papery		OT	Initial stage of staling, bready (stale bread crumb), cardboard, old beer, oxidized	(5-Methylfurfural, 25 mg/L)
	0830 Leathery		OTM	Later stage of staling, often used in conjunction with 0211 Woody	
	0840 Moldy		OT	Cellarlike, leaf mold, woodsy	
		0841 Earthy	OT	Actinomycetes, damp soil, freshly dug soil, diatomaceous earth	(Geosmin)
		0842 Musty	OT	Fusty	

Class 9 — Sour, Acidic

Class Term	First Tier	Second Tier	Relevance	Comments, Synonyms, Definitions	Reference Standard
0900 Acidic			OT	Pungent aroma, sharpness of taste, mineral acid	
	0910 Acetic		OT	vinegar	(Acetic acid)
	0920 Sour		OT	Lactic, sour milk; use with 0141 Citrus for citrus-sour	

Class Term	First Tier	Second Tier	Relevance	Comments, Synonyms, Definitions	Reference Standard
Class 10 — Sweet					
1000 Sweet			OT		Sucrose, 7.5 g/L
	1001 Honey		OT	Can occur as effect of beer staling (e.g. odor of stale beer in glass), oxidized (stale) honey	
	1002 Jamlike		OT	May be qualified by subclasses of 0140 Fruity	
	1003 Vanilla		OT	Custard powder, vanillin	(Vanillin)
	1004 Primings		OT		
	1005 Syrupy		OTM	clear (golden) syrup	
	1006 Oversweet		OT	Sickly sweet, cloying	
Class 11 — Salty					
1100 Salty			T		Sodium chloride, 1.8 g/L
Class 12 — Bitter					
1200 Bitter			TAf		(Isohumulone)
Class 13 — Mouthfeel					
	1310 Alkaline		TMAf	Flavor imparted by accidental admixture of alkaline detergent	(Sodium bicarbonate)
	1320 Mouthcoating		MAf	Creamy, onctueux (Fr.)	
	1330 Metallic		OTMAf	Iron, rusty water, coins, tinny, inky	(Ferrous ammonium sulfate)
	1340 Astringent		MAf	Mouth puckering, puckery, tanninlike, tart	Quercitrin, 240 mg/L
		1341 Drying	MAf	Unsweet	
	1350 Powdery		OTM	O — Dusty cushion, irritating, (with 0310 Grainy) mill-room smell TM — Chalky, particulate, scratchy, silicatelike, siliceous	

Class Term	First Tier	Second Tier	Relevance	Comments, Synonyms, Definitions	Reference Standard
	1360 Carbonation		M	CO_2 content	
		1361 Flat	M	Undercarbonated	60% of normal CO_2 content for the product
		1362 Gassy	M	Overcarbonated	140% of normal CO_2 content for the product
	1370 Warming		WMAf	See 0110 Alcoholic and 0111 Spicy	
Class 14 — Fullness					
	1410 Body		OTM	Fullness of flavor and mouthfeel	
		1411 Watery	TM	Thin, seemingly diluted	
		1412 Characterless	OTM	Bland, empty, flavorless	
		1413 Satiating	OTM	Extra full, filling	
		1414 Thick	TM	Viscous, *epais* (Fr.)	

Quercitrin is both astringent and bitter.

Reprinted with permission from *Journal of the American Society of Brewing Chemists, Inc.*, 1979.

TESTING YOURSELF

CHARLIE PAPAZIAN

I t's a rough job, but someone's got to do it." As judges of beer we may joke about our predicament. After all, the beer we are drinking is meant to be enjoyed. So often we are in that enviable position of having to taste many beers, perhaps ten, fifteen, or heaven forbid, twenty beers. Sounds great, doesn't it?

I enjoy judging and evaluating beers because it is a continually challenging exercise. I've been evaluating beer as a judge and tastemaster for more than ten years. I've been evaluating my own beer for more than fifteen years. I've become a better brewer primarily because I've made the effort to learn how to constructively evaluate other people's beer and use what I've learned on my own efforts. I'm still learning.

Accurately evaluating beer does not come easy. It takes dedication, training, years of practice and a very wide variety of beer experiences. Those of you who are homebrewers have an advantage; you know the process and understand where flavors originate once you learn how to identify them.

If you want to learn how to evaluate beer, you have your wort cut out for you. There are more than 850 chemical compounds that occur naturally in the fermentation process (see *zymurgy* Summer 1982, Vol. 5, No. 2). Many hundreds of these compounds remain in the beer or change to something else with time and condition. These compounds titillate the tens of thousands of taste buds on our tongue. The resulting symphony is the taste we nonchalantly identify as beer flavor.

We find ourselves attempting to isolate and identify one of a few flavors among hundreds. How our brain manages to do this is a wonder still not fully understood. With the desire we can train ourselves to learn; first, how to recognize a type of flavor, then second, how to perceive various intensities of particular flavors. The final test and the most difficult, is to recognize, perceive and isolate a number of flavors among many in our glass of beer.

As homebewers, our impressive goal is not only to evaluate beer flavor but to identify or postulate their origins. We have to isolate desirable beer flavors from undesirable beer flavors and, like a detective, track down the origins and make adjustments in the brewing process, choice of ingredients, handling, etc. Our goals are noble indeed.

However, the most noble of all is to evaluate someone else's beer, to accurately and constructively assist them with the ultimate end of improving the quality of homebrew everywhere. This is the noblest of all ambitions and it is what judging homebrew competitions is all about.

How does one begin learning to evaluate beer? The answer is patience, practice, humility, practice, time, practice, training and more practice. If you want to learn how to evaluate beer, understand that every person's abilities are different. Not all of us have the same ability to perceive flavors. For some it will seem to come naturally. For others it will take persistence, practice and personal guidance. Don't be discouraged if you can't taste what other people can. Simply continue to enjoy your beer and leave the job of evaluation to others with the ability. Believe it or not, some people's senses cannot perceive certain flavors.

GETTING STARTED

Let's take a look at the elements of flavor perception and then consider some options you have for training yourself or a group of people in the art of beer flavor evaluation.

The sensory experience of taste begins with the tongue. We perceive four principal types of sensations: sweet, sour, bitter and salty. Sweetness is only perceived at the tip of the tongue. Salt and sour are perceived on both sides and finally, as food or drink make their way to the back of the tongue we perceive bitter. When people speak of bitterness or sourness, many are confused. Understanding the "mapping" of the tongue serves to get everyone perceiving and expressing their perceptions the same way.

When tasting beer, serve at temperatures no cooler than 50 degrees F (10 degrees C), preferably 50 to 60 degrees F (10 to 15.5 degrees C) for ales. Move the beer to all parts of your tongue to experience the flavor sensations properly. When conducting a tasting, the serving cups should be spotlessly clean, odorless and identical. This is essential to eliminate bias.

Many (but not all) of the following formulas are taken from brewing papers presented by Morten Meilgaard (director of brewing at the Stroh Brewing Company) to the American Society of Brewing Chemists.

The following formulas are good for making sixty-four fluid ounces (two quarts or nearly one six-pack of 12-ounce bottles) of tasting solution. This is adequate for a group of 30 people, each receiving a two-ounce serving. To formulate these "recipes" you will need some special measuring devices:

1. A five-milliliter glass pipette
2. A safety pipette filler
3. A gram scale that will measure accurately to one-tenth of a gram
4. A glass measuring cup, graduated in ounces. Small gram scales and glass pipettes are relatively inexpensive and can be bought at any chemical laboratory supply house.

Illustration by Vicki Hopewell

To train yourself or others to perceive the four basic flavors here are some formulas:

In two quarts of distilled water at room temperature add: 38 grams of white table sugar for sweet; 0.95 grams of tartaric acid for sour; 9.5 grams of table salt (sodium chloride) for salty; and 2.85 grams of caffeine for bitterness or 6 milliliters of the following stock solution for bitterness:

To make stock solution of isohop extract mix 3 milliliters of isohop extract with 100 milliliters of distilled water. Isomerized hop extract is extremely bitter and must be diluted.

A fifth elemental sensation important to beer evaluators is the sensation of astringency, the dry puckery sensation of tannin: 1.9 grams of tannic acid (grape tannin) for astringency. This experience can also be achieved by eating a red grape and chewing on the skin for a long time.

Both tartaric acid and tannin can be found at winemaking supply stores. Caffeine can be found at chemical supply outlet.

TEST YOURSELF FOR INTENSITY PERCEPTION

Concoct the following recipes in the following proportions and conduct a tasting where the taster is not aware which samples are more intense than the other. Ask them to rate intensity.

In each 12-ounce bottle of light American Pilsener beer add:

For sweet: 1.8 grams sugar
3.5 grams sugar
5.31 grams sugar

For salty: 0.4 grams salt (NaCl)
0.8 grams salt (NaCl)
1.2 grams salt (NaCl)

This will demonstrate the effect of the excessive addition of brewing salts, particularly Burton water treatment, brewing or water crystals, which may have sodium chloride and magnesium sulfate (epsom salt), both salty in flavor.

For sour: Make a stock solution that is 16 percent lactic acid and 84 percent distilled water. Lactic acid is packaged in various strengths. You will have to do some math to get to the desired dilution. Concentrated liquid lactic acid can be bought at wine and beer supply stores or at most pharmacies.

CAUTION: Use protective glasses when working with concentrated lactic acids and read cautionary instructions on container.

For sour: 1 ml of 16 percent stock solution
2 ml of 15 percent stock solution
4 ml of 16 percent stock solution

This will demonstrate one of the effects of bacterial contamination.

For bitter: zero milliliters of isohop stock solution (see above)
3 milliliters of isohop stock solution
5 milliliters of isohop stock solution

This will demonstrate the bitter character that hops can contribute.

TEST YOUR DESCRIPTIVE ABILITY

Here are a few flavor characters common in beer that you can safely formulate.

Caramellike flavor (equivalent to 2 pounds per 5 gallons): For demonstrating the sweet caramellike flavor and beer body builder, steep 0.2 pounds of crushed crystal malt in 2.25 quarts of 150- to 160-degree-F (65.5- to 71-degree-C) water for 45 minutes. Strain and bottle "crystal malt extract." Keep cool or refrigerate and plan to serve at room temperature within two days.

Black malt flavor (equivalent to 0.5 pounds per 5 gallons): To demonstrate the charcoallike, carbonized sharp bitter flavor contributed by black malt, steep 0.05 pounds of black malt in 2.25 quarts 150- to 160-degree-F (65.5- to 71-degree-C) water for 45 minutes. Strain and bottle "black malt extract." Keep cool or refrigerate and plan to serve at room temperature within two days.

Roast barley flavor (equivalent to 0.5 pounds per 5 gallons): For demonstrating the essential roasted coffeelike flavor in stouts, steep 0.05 pounds of roasted barley in 2.25 quarts 150- to 160-degree-F (65.5- to 71-degree-C) water for 45 minutes. Strain and bottle "roast barley extract." Keep cool or refrigerate and plan to serve at room temperature within two days.

Hop aroma (equivalent to 0.5 ounce dry hopping in 5 gallons): Steep 1 gram of Cascade hop pellets in 2 quarts of cold water for two to three days. Strain and bottle. This sample is for perceiving aroma only.

Grainy husklike astringent flavor (equivalent to 2 pounds in 5 gallons): For demonstrating the undesirable characteristic of boiled grains, boil 0.2 pounds of crushed crystal malt in 2.25 quarts of water for 45 minutes. Strain and bottle "crystal malt extract." Keep cool or refrigerate and plan to serve at room temperature within two days. For best demonstration, serve side by side with steeped caramel malt extract.

MORE FLAVOR CHARACTERS

Flavor characters you can add to 12-ounce bottles of light American Pilsener style beer.

Note: Whenever serving the following samples serve them side by side with a "control" bottle of untainted Pilsener beer of the same variety as the flavored sample.

Alcoholic: To demonstrate the warming sensation and the mouthfeel and flavor of high alcohol beers such as bocks, doppelbocks, barley wines, and other strong beers. To boost the alcoholic content of a 12-ounce bottle of beer by 5 percent by volume remove 19 milliliters of beer and replace them with 19 milliliters of grain (180 proof alcohol) or similarly with 36 milliliters of 80 proof vodka.

Skunklike aroma and flavor: To demonstrate the effects of improper handling; specifically, short exposure to direct sunlight or long exposure to fluorescent light will create a photochemical reaction with hops in the beer. Clear or green bottles afford no protection. Brown glass helps, though not entirely.

Set bottles of beer in sunlight for twelve hours.

Oxidized: Papery/
Sherrylike aroma
and flavor: To demonstrate the effects of oxygen on the shelf life of beer; particularly of beer that is not kept refrigerated. This is a common characteristic with many "well-aged" homebrews.

Chill beer to near freezing. Pour into another clean bottle. The objective is to introduce some air (oxygen) while not creating excess foaming. Recap and "incubate" bottles at 100 degrees F (38 degrees C) for seven days. Setting it on or near your furnace or hot water heater may be adequate. Be sure to have a control bottle of beer to compare with this sample.

Formulation of the above flavor samples is done by an individual trained in handling the samples. Incredibly small amounts are used in some of these formulations.

OTHER FLAVORS

There are many more common beer flavors that can be demonstrated with similar formulation. Some of the more commonly demonstrated flavors are:

Buttery or
diacetyl (created by bacteria or improper yeast fermentation).

Banana or (created by warm fermentations and particular
solventlike strains of brewing yeast).

Hydrogen
sulfide (H_2S)
or rotten egg (created by certain strains of yeast).

Metallic or (created by excessive cleaning of metal brewpots,
bloodlike flavor exposed steel in enameled pots or some grades of aluminum.

Sweet cornlike
flavor or DMS,
dimethyl sulfide (created by the slow cooling of the wort).

TRAINING SESSIONS

There is a lot to learn. It should be emphasized that it does take practice, especially when judging the real thing, beer. Organize your training sessions beforehand and don't try to do too much at one time.

For any size group, a sampling and discussion of six to eight types of flavors or their combination can easily take the better part of two hours. You will want to discuss what you and your colleagues are experiencing and how it is applied to beer and homebrewing.

These flavors are common to commercial as well as homebrewed beers. Because they are brewed under varied conditions, homebrewed beers offer the opportunity to exhibit many more flavor variations.

If you're to become a qualified homebrew judge you may find yourself in the position of trying to detect bacterial sourness in an already naturally sour fruit beer. Or how about trying to catch the hop aroma in a licorice-flavored garlic stout. Remember: be patient, be constructive and practice.

It's a rough job but someone has to do it.

Copyright 1986 Charlie Papazian

SOURCES

"Evaluating Beer," Charlie Papazian, *zymurgy*, Winter 1990 (Vol. 13, No. 5).

"The Flavor of Beer," Morten C. Meilgaard, *MBAA Technical Quarterly, Vol. 28, 1991.*

"The Sensory Aspects of Zymological Evaluation," David W. Eby, *zymurgy*, Winter 1992 (Vol. 15, No. 5)

"Sensory Evaluation for Brewers," Jean-Xavier Guinard and Ian Robertson, *Beer and Brewing, Vol. 8*, Brewers Publications, 1988.

"Beer Flavor in Your Brewery," Ron Siebel, *Brewery Operations, Vol. 3*, Brewers Publications, 1987.

"Origins of Normal and Abnormal Flavor," Ted Konis, *Beer and Brewing, Vol. 6*, Brewers Publications, 1987.

"Flavor Profiles," Ilse Shelton, *Brewery Operations, Vol. 9*, Brewers Publications, 1992.

"Training Ourselves in Flavor Perception and Tasting," Raoul Palamand is a combination of two articles,

"Training Ourselves in Flavor Perception," *Beer and Brewing, Vol. 6*, Brewers Publications, 1986 and **"Origins of Desirable and Undesirable Beer Flavors,"** *Brewery Operations, Vol. 4*, Brewers Publications, 1988.

"A Simple Technique for Evaluating Beer Color," George Fix, *zymurgy*, Fall 1988 (Vol. 11, No. 3).

"The Language of Flavor Communication," Charlie Papazian, *Beer and Brewing, Vol. 6*, Brewers Publications, 1986.

"What to Aim for in Flavor Profiling," Charlie Papazian, *zymurgy*, Special Issue 1987 (Vol. 10, No. 4).

"Beer Evaluation Techniques," Grosvenor Merle-Smith, *Beer and Brewing, Vol. 7*, Brewers Publications, 1987.

"Perceiving Flavor," Jim Koch, *Beer and Brewing, Vol. 7*, Brewers Publications, 1987.

"Know Your Consumer Through Testing," Morten C. Meilgaard, *The New Brewer*, November-December 1992 (Vol. 9, No. 6).

"Aroma Identification," Charlie Papazian and Greg Noonan, *Beer and Brewing, Vol. 8*, Brewers Publications, 1988. **Flavor Wheel and Beer Flavor Terminology Chart** by Morten C. Meilgaard, D.Sc., F.I. Brew.

"Testing Yourself," Charlie Papazian, *zymurgy*, Spring 1986 (Vol. 9, No. 1).

AUTHOR BIOGRAPHIES

DAVID W. EBY received his masters and doctorate from the University of California, Santa Barbara in experimental psychology. He has completed a post-doctorate at the University of California, Irvine, in visual perception. Presently he is in the Department of Psychology at California State University — San Bernadino. Since beginning to homebrew in 1981, David has entered numerous AHA competitions. He enjoys science fiction, sports and art.

A native Texan, **GEORGE FIX** lives with his wife Laurie in Arlington. He earned a doctorate at Harvard University and has been on the faculties of Harvard, Michigan and Carnegie-Mellon. He is chairman of the mathematics department at the University of Texas at Arlington, senior consultant for Brewers Research and Development Co., a quality control consultant for Crosby and Baker, author of *Principles of Brewing Science*, and co-author of *Vienna, Märzen, Oktoberfest* (Brewers Publications, 1989, 1992). George has won 60 brewing awards.

JEAN-XAVIER GUINARD is an assistant professor in the Department of Nutrition at Penn State University where he teaches and conducts research on taste and the sensory properties of foods, including beer.

He obtained his doctorate in microbiology at the University of California at Davis Brewing Laboratory under Michael Lewis. Jean-Xavier has published various research papers on the sensory properties of beer and is author of *Lambic* by Brewers Publications.

JIM KOCH, founder of the Boston Beer Co. and brewer, is a sixth-generation brewer. Harvard-educated, Jim left his management consultant job in 1984 to resurrect his great-great grandfather's lager recipe, which he renamed Samuel Adams Boston Lager. Jim's Samuel Adams has gone on to win much acclaim and numerous awards, including being named "Best Brew of the Decade" by *Time Magazine* in 1990 and twice winning first place in the Great American Beer Festival's popular poll.

TED KOHIS is senior brewing consultant at the Siebel Institute in Chicago, Ill., where he has been employed for 20 years. He has more than 30 years of experience in the brewing industry starting as a research technician with Miller Brewing Co. in 1959. In 1961 he joined the Carling Brewing Co. where he worked for 10 years eventually becoming brewmaster of the Cleveland plant. Ted has degrees in chemistry and biology and has done advanced work in biochemistry.

MORTEN C. MEILGAARD, D.SC., F.I. BREW., is a world renowned, international consultant in sensory analysis and food science and technology. He is also senior technical adviser to the Stroh Brewery Co. in Detroit, Mich., where he served from 1982 to 1989 as VP of Research. He is best known for his role in the design of the Flavor Wheel for beer and the book, *Sensory Analysis Techniques* (CRC Press).

GROSVENOR MERLE-SMITH was vice president of the Association of Brewers in Boulder, Colo., between 1983 and 1988 and served on the Board of Directors. He directed the AHA National Homebrew Competition from 1984 to 1987. Grosvenor taught beer evaluation classes and helped create the AHA and Home Wine Beer Trade Association Beer Judge Certification Program. He is currently hunting a pack of fox hounds in Virginia.

GREGORY NOONAN is brewmaster at the Vermont Pub and Brewery in Burlington, Vt., and author of *Brewing Lager Beer* and *Scotch Ale* (Brewers Publications 1986, 1993). He has written numerous articles in brewing periodicals, including a series on beer styles for *The New Brewer*.

RAOUL PALAMAND, PH.D., of St. Louis, Mo., is president of Summit Products Inc., a consulting firm serving the beverage industry. He has more than 25 years of experience in the beverage industry specializing in product development, flavor formulation, analysis and trouble shooting. Raoul taught flavor chemistry at Southern Illinois University in Edwardsville for five years and served as director of new product development at Anheuser-Busch for more than twelve years where he was responsible for introducing a number of alcoholic and non-alcoholic beverages.

CHARLIE PAPAZIAN is the founder and president of the Association of Brewers and author of *The New Complete Joy of Home Brewing* (Avon 1991). Charlie is an allied member of the Master Brewer Association of the Americas as well as an active member of the American Society of Brewing Chemists.

IAN ROBERTSON earned his B.S. in food science in 1986 and in 1989 he began working for Anheuser-Busch in Fairfield, Calif., as a microbiology intern. After a year with Anheuser-Busch he worked for a biotechnical company, California Truffle Co., which was developing technology for large scale production of French Perigord truffles. Following that experience, Ian worked for a year at Kohnan Inc., a saké brewery in the Napa Valley, in quality control, fermentation research, and new product development. Ian completed his masters in food science in 1992 and now is attending the University of California in San Francisco studying for his doctorate of pharmacy.

ILSE SHELTON is vice president of Laboratory. Services at J.E. Siebel Sons' Co. and an instructor at the Siebel Institute for Technology where she trains students in the sensory evaluation of beer. She joined Siebel in 1989 as manager of analytical services. Previously, she was the supervisor for the chemical analysis laboratory at John Labatt, Ltd. in Canada.

RON SIEBEL is president of J.E. Siebel Sons' Co. and is the fourth generation of his family to serve as the corporation president. He joined the company in 1966 after graduating from the University of Miami. In 1967 he graduated from the Siebel Institute and apprenticed at Molson's Brewery in Montreal, after which he worked in small United States breweries nationwide.

INDEX

HOMEBREWER?

Join the thousands of American Homebrewers Association members who read **zymurgy** — the magazine for homebrewers and beer lovers.

Every issue of **zymurgy** is full of tips, techniques, new recipes, new products, equipment and ingredient reviews, beer news, technical articles — the whole world of homebrewing. PLUS, the AHA brings members the National Homebrewers Conference, the National Homebrew Competition, the Beer Judge Certification Program, the Homebrew Club Network, periodic discounts on books from Brewers Publications and much much more.

Photocopy and mail this coupon today to join the AHA or call now for credit card orders, (303) 546-6514.

Name

Address

City   State/Province

Zip/Postal Code   Country

Phone

☐ Enclosed is $29 for one full year.
Canadian memberships are $34 US, Foreign memberships are $44 US.

☐ Please charge my credit card ☐ Visa ☐ MC

Card No.   —   —   —   Exp. Date

Signature

Make check to: American Homebrewers Association, PO Box 1510, Boulder, CO 80306 USA
Offer valid until 12/31/94.   Prices subject to change.   BP093

BOOKS for Brewers and Beer Lovers

Order Now ... Your Brew Will Thank You!

These books offered by Brewers Publications are some of the most sought after reference tools for homebrewers and professional brewers alike. Filled with tips, techniques, recipes and history, these books will help you expand your brewing horizons. Let the world's foremost brewers help you as you brew. So whatever your brewing level or interest, Brewers Publications has the information necessary for you to brew the best beer in the world — your beer.

- -

Please send me more free information on the following: (check all that apply)

◇ Merchandise & Book Catalog
◇ American Homebrewers Association
◇ Institute for Brewing Studies
◇ Great American Beer Festival℠

Ship to:

Name

Address

City   State/Province

Zip/Postal Code   Country

Daytime Phone   (   )

Payment Method

◇ Check or Money Order Enclosed (Payable to the Association of Brewers)
◇ Visa   ◇ MasterCard

Card Number   −   −   −   Expiration Date

Name on Card   Signature

Brewers Publications, PO Box 1679, Boulder, CO 80306-1679, (303) 546-6514, FAX (303) 447-2825.

BP-O93

BREWERS PUBLICATIONS ORDER FORM

PROFESSIONAL BREWING BOOKS

QTY.	TITLE	STOCK #	PRICE	EXT. PRICE
_____	Brewery Planner..440		.80.00	_____
_____	North American Brewers Resource Directory...............451		..80.00	_____
_____	Principles of Brewing Science....................................415		..29.95	_____

THE BREWERY OPERATIONS SERIES
from Micro and Pubbrewers Conferences

QTY.	TITLE	STOCK #	PRICE	EXT. PRICE
_____	Volume 4, 1987 Conference..424		..25.95	_____
_____	Volume 5, 1988 Conference..428		..25.95	_____
_____	Volume 6, 1989 Conference..430		..25.95	_____
_____	Volume 7, 1990 Conference..433		..25.95	_____
_____	Volume 8, 1991 Conference,			
	Brewing Under Adversity...442		..25.95	_____
_____	Volume 9, 1992 Conference,			
	Quality Brewing — Share the Experience...............447		..25.95	_____

CLASSIC BEER STYLE SERIES

QTY.	TITLE	STOCK #	PRICE	EXT. PRICE
_____	Pale Ale 431		..11.95	_____
_____	Continental Pilsener 434		..11.95	_____
_____	Lambic..437		..11.95	_____
_____	Vienna, Märzen, Oktoberfest...............................444		..11.95	_____
_____	Porter...443		..11.95	_____
_____	Belgian Ale 446		..11.95	_____
_____	German Wheat Beer..448		..11.95	_____
_____	Scotch Ale 449		..11.95	_____
_____	Bock (available Spring 1994)..................................452		..11.95	_____

BEER AND BREWING SERIES, for homebrewers and beer enthusiasts
from National Homebrewers Conferences

QTY.	TITLE	STOCK #	PRICE	EXT. PRICE
_____	Volume 8, 1988 Conference..427		..21.95	_____
_____	Volume 9, 1989 Conference..429		..21.95	_____
_____	Volume 10, 1990 Conference......................................432		..21.95	_____
_____	Volume 11, 1991 Conference, Brew Free Or Die!.........435		..21.95	_____
_____	Volume 12, 1992 Conference, Just Brew It!..................436		..21.95	_____

GENERAL BEER AND BREWING INFORMATION

QTY.	TITLE	STOCK #	PRICE	EXT. PRICE
_____	Brewing Lager Beer..417		..14.95	_____
_____	Brewing Mead..418		..11.95	_____
_____	Dictionary of Beer and Brewing 414		..19.95	_____
_____	Evaluating Beer...456		..25.95	_____
_____	Great American Beer Cookbook...................................455		..24.95	_____
_____	Winners Circle 407		..11.95	_____

Call or write for a free *Beer Enthusiast* catalog today.
- U.S. funds only.
- All Brewers Publications books come with a money-back guarantee.
- *Postage & Handling: $3 for the first book ordered, plus $1 for each book thereafter. Canadian and foreign orders please add $4 for the first book and $2 for each book thereafter. Orders cannot be shipped without appropriate P&H.

SUBTOTAL _____
Colo. Residents Add
3% Sales Tax _____
P & H * _____
TOTAL _____

Brewers Publications, PO Box 1679, Boulder, CO 80306-1679, (303) 546-6514, FAX (303) 447-2825.

BP-O93

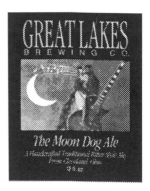